IMAGE
CONTROL

SOCIAL MEDIA, FASCISM, AND THE

DISMANTLING OF DEMOCRACY

PATRICK NATHAN

COUNTERPOINT
BERKELEY, CALIFORNIA

Image Control

Copyright © 2021 by Patrick Nathan
First hardcover edition: 2021
First paperback edition: 2022

The Library of Congress has cataloged the hardcover edition as follows:
Names: Nathan, Patrick, author.
Title: Image control : art, fascism, and the right to resist / Patrick Nathan.
Description: Berkeley, California : Counterpoint, 2021.
Identifiers: LCCN 2020047991 | ISBN 9781640094536 (hardcover) | ISBN 9781640094543
    (ebook)
Subjects: LCSH: Propaganda. | Images, Photographic—Social aspects. | Fascism.
Classification: LCC HM1231 .N38 2021 | DDC 303.3/75—dc23
LC record available at https://lccn.loc.gov/202004799

Paperback ISBN: 978-1-64009-554-0

Cover design by Dana Li
Book design by Jordan Koluch

COUNTERPOINT
2560 Ninth Street, Suite 318
Berkeley, CA 94710
www.counterpointpress.com

Printed in the United States of America

10 9 8 7 6 5 4 3 2 1

Praise for *Image Control*

ALSO BY PATRICK NATHAN

Some Hell

For my friends

Darren Rovell ✓
@darrenrovell

i feel bad for our country. But this is tremendous content.

9:21 PM · Oct 19, 2016 · TweetDeck

2.6K Retweets **6.1K** Likes

CONTENTS

INTRODUCTION

LET THEM EAT A PLAGUE

The fence was a place to hang our roses but it's gone now, dismantled and cast into a ravine. To confuse visitors, the roads have new names. But anyone can find the photograph: the rails and wooden X's at what looks to be sunrise, shot so they tower over the rocks and dirt and prairie grass. It's meant to look desolate. The fence's blush among the blue of morning is meant to evoke the windchill of eastern Wyoming. Published on the cover of *Time* in October 1998, Steve Liss's photo tries to say, "A murder like Matthew Shepard's must never happen again." Ultimately, it's a beautiful photograph. Ultimately, like any photograph, it can't say anything at all.

Once, I thought it could. To me, that photograph said how it would feel to flirt with two strangers, only to be taken and beaten and left to die alone in the night. I thought it said, *This is what happens if they find out.* But photographs don't speak. They don't demand or insist or chastise, despite a strange and pervasive assumption that they should. With social media and digital photography, this assumption—that images have meaning—is both widespread and increasingly dangerous. In ceding to photographs and other images the kind of authority that belongs to language, we risk destabilizing our relationships not only with one another but with reality itself.

Assuming that images can speak—that we can, as with social media, use them in substitution for what we wish to say to others—is what opens the door to fascism, an ideology that requires a schism with reality. If we begin replacing our language with images, it is fascism that will finish this process—that will replace reality itself, including the reality of human beings.

I never thought I'd write a book about photographs and fascism because I knew nothing, I thought, about photographs and fascism. These are realms of what is called expertise, a term meant to dissuade those who seek to educate or inform themselves without borrowing large sums of money. This is the trap of "none of my business," in which we surrender authority over what is indeed our business: living our lives alongside others. In our relationships with one another, with technology, with public health, and with government, there is no objective or neutral. In place of objectivity or neutrality, there is, it turns out, right and wrong, and it is both disastrous and immoral to allow what is wrong to perpetuate simply because it falls under someone else's intellectual or professional jurisdiction.

Seeing is the primary metaphor for human understanding, for being in the world. But it's only a metaphor. In his *Confessions*, Saint Augustine observed (that is, he "saw") how we don't use the other senses to describe sight: "We do not say, hark how it flashes, or smell how it glows, or taste how it shines, or feel how it gleams; for all these are said to be seen." But we do say, "See how it soundeth, see how it smelleth, see how it tasteth, see how hard it is." It's tempting to interpret, as Augustine does, this primacy of sight as the presence of the divine. It is, after all, what is divine—derived from *dyeu*, "to shine"—that brings light and makes sight possible. It is God, as Augustine knows, who let there be light, whatever God may be.

I mention Genesis as a work of literature, a shared story—

one that places concepts like light and seeing and existence in context. It narrates the separation of the world into forms—not only where *this* meets *that* but how they came into being. While not religious, I refer to Christianity as one of many common moral frameworks that remind us of the ethical responsibilities of being human. One of these responsibilities is to see or try to see things, people, and situations as they are: where they end and begin, how they attach themselves to others, and how they are presented and represented to those who are meant to see or not see them. This has nothing to do with isolated images and everything to do with how they connect or relate. If the cliché "seeing is believing" carries any merit, it is definitely not in a world where we view the image as a kind of currency for consuming or collecting information. It is by misunderstanding "seeing is believing" that the fascist imagination—predicated on division, isolation, and elimination—takes hold.

And these are fascist times. I don't know whether to be grateful or alarmed that no one, any longer, calls me hysterical for saying this. And while the most visible aspect of this fascism is, without a doubt, an omnipresent, autocratic bigot whose every photograph and tweet and facial gesture is consumed and interpreted in myriad ways—a kind of image-meth scarcely anyone can stop using—to call Donald Trump this fascism's alpha and omega is to give him too much credit. If anything, he's just a mutant created from our nuclear waste, a C.H.U.D. from the political sewers we could no longer keep hidden underground. Outside the White House, fascism runs as deep as America itself, and—following the river of corpses floating atop the Atlantic—back into Europe and European history. Individuals in society learned to treat one another like images, like objects to collect or discard, long before some mediocre idiot made it a national platform. Part of undoing this, of resisting this, is to understand it.

In American mythology, the story goes, we are not here to be protected. But we are free to protect ourselves. Isn't that our "right," as citizens of the United States? Doesn't each of us have the freedom to draw a line, to place a boundary on how much of ourselves we choose to give or risk? Isn't it a "choice" to work or not work, to make money or remain poor? To maintain a "healthy lifestyle" or get sick? In American life and art, the individual is the nexus of choice—of risk, of pain, of joy, of incomparable punishments or rewards. More anciently, Christianity calls this "free will," which so often translates into fault, into blame. With respect to our freedoms or rights in America, so much of what is narrated—in art and in politics—is our isolation. Fascism's lodestar is loneliness.

Somewhat recently, we perhaps saw this most clearly in the early days of the coronavirus pandemic, an information-event rich with unique and interpretable (that is, meaningless) images. "In an epidemic," Elias Canetti writes in *Crowds and Power*, "people *see* the advance of death; it takes place under their very eyes." But in those days we saw few, if any, American bodies piling up in journalistic photographs—certainly nothing like the corpses newspapers showed us a few years earlier, when Ebola struck several West African nations. Instead, we saw voids. In Italy and New York, the famously packed museums were deserted. In Beijing, home to twenty-one million people, the streets were empty. Nobody was at the Louvre or the Eiffel Tower, and in the subway stations of dense cities worldwide, one might've heard a pin drop. Looking at them now, these images recall apocalyptic films depicting cityscapes and interiors after the imagined collapse of civilization, or even photographs of real places now abandoned by human inhabitants, such as Matthew Christopher's images from the Chernobyl Exclusion

Zone or Yves Marchand's images of libraries, theaters, schools, and train stations in Detroit.

But they also don't resemble them, not quite. A ruin is ravaged, sometimes by war, usually by time. Ruins are human-made structures fallen into disrepair. Yet nothing in the images of empty cities and museums is destroyed or crumbling. In Alessandro Grassani's photograph from March 2020, published on the front page of *The New York Times*, thirty-two small, identical plastic chairs are spaced six feet apart in the massive baroque courtyard of the Palazzo Marino in Milan. *Measures are being taken*, the photograph, if we were to read it, might suggest. Yet that the chairs are empty—that even they, medicinally distant from one another, are void of human beings—suggests these measures will fail.

Instead of disease or nuclear war or even climate change, these photographs of emptiness suggest that we simply disappeared. In those days, with our public spaces erased of people, everyone in physical isolation could look at a newspaper or magazine or computer screen and feel like the last person on earth.

Of course, these deserted spaces appeared alongside other, more familiar and immediate images of emptiness: ransacked shelves. Not only was there a sudden lack of options after a lifetime of redundant plenitude, but we *saw*, repeatedly, this scarcity. The emptiness had arrived in our cities, in our own neighborhoods, in our marketplaces. We could no longer buy or sell what we used to freely buy and sell: what was really dying, these images seemed to say, was a certain transactional way of life.

This was reinforced by various calls to consumption, themselves images of normalcy, of how to "survive" (assimilate) a pandemic. Amid self-imposed quarantine or stay-at-home orders lurked a sense of consumerist opportunity: *Waiting out the virus? A book blog has recommendations for you. A magazine wants you to make these soups. An app invites you to learn a new language.* It was the perfect time, a retail chain nagged me in one email, to tackle those household projects I'd been ignoring. Never mind that laid-off workers were perhaps not in the mood to shop, or that parents had to homeschool their children, or that some families had to take care of sick and ailing relatives. Never mind that most adults working from home inevitably found their working hours spread over the whole of the day in an "office" they could never leave.

Meanwhile, a magazine said, "We'll get through COVID-19 together"—especially if you subscribe. "It's a *hard* time," quipped a sex toy retailer—a great reason to spend money. "What you need now," a newspaper threatened, "is the truth." Whether to instill apocalyptic dread or convince us to keep calm and carry on shopping, it should shock no one how quickly a global pandemic was assimilated as content. The virus gave every commercial entity a reason to reach out, to check on consumers. The more emotional the tone, the better, be it a mournful note about family or a joke about missing all that dick you used to get. Even the imagination of apocalypse, it turned out, could be personalized, branded, and marketed to specific demographics.

That COVID-19 would be an occasion for personal consumption and a source of daily entertainment via memes, language games, and jokes was inevitable. *Something*, after all, must fill the space left empty by the restaurants and bars that once defined our nights and weekends, by the clothes we'd bought for others to notice, and above all by images of our own we could no longer share—images of food we didn't prepare, of drinks we didn't make, of ourselves smiling in faraway places our friends and followers may never be able to afford to visit themselves.

If we aren't, after all, experiencing desires and making overt, visible choices based on those desires, are we still us? Am I, without perpetually modulating my lifestyle, still me?

***

Like images, illnesses mean nothing. The attempt to interpret COVID-19, to build meaning around it—to ask what it can teach us, what it reveals about us—has nothing to do with the virus itself and everything to do with how nations, corporations, and individuals chose to react to it. So too with images. The photographs of vacant streets and shelves, then and now, mean nothing. They are not messages, diagnoses, prognostications, or warnings. All images rely on context—where we see them, how we see them, and who has shown them to us.

Being trapped at home was, we were told, a "surreal" moment. The empty streets and shelves were surreal. It's a word Americans often reach for when something destabilizes the ongoing transactions of daily life, when life seems not itself. This life almost always means one's role within the economy. To be pushed into surreality in America is to suddenly notice the strangeness of one's relationship to producing and consuming. It is at last to narrate for oneself, *This is really my life and this is how I'm living it.*

In 1966, Max Kozloff, a critic at *Artforum*, distinguished Surrealism from its ideological contemporary, Expressionism: "Whereas Expressionism wanted to wrest the viewer's involvement into the rhythms of violent paint handling, Surrealism . . . sought to engage him with the visualized spectacle of his inner life." This suggests a direct line connecting the immense and lasting popularity of the surrealist ethos with how capitalism, by isolating and aggrandizing the importance of individual choice and desire in every relationship we have, depletes us of the capacity for an inner life.

Surrealism, Kozloff argues, "opens up the possibility of a wholeness and personal integration on a behavioral level from which its artistic embodiment will only seem to trail behind." Today, that "integration on a behavioral level" manifests as a near constant stream of individualistic content meant for public consumption, mined from the recesses of the personal. These are the fragments we broadcast to followers as well as those we scroll through, an algorithmically sorted, polyvocal stream of consciousness that always promises, but never offers, coherence. Our social media timelines are always, it seems, *just about* to mean. What surrealism explored in art for individuals to contemplate—*Here is the total contents of the artist's inner life; make of it what you will*—social media now encourages everyone to practice, not as art but as daily, self-guided distraction: here are the contents of my thoughts, shattered into isolated units and mixed alongside yours and everyone else's, like coins at the bottom of a well.

In surrealist thinking, the imagination of existence is not unified, interrelated, continuous, imbricated, or ongoing. It is instead atomized into interchangeable units. Despite their appearance together, your thoughts and mine—your life and mine—are not imagined as related. Similar to surrealist paintings, novels, or films, these inner lives are presented in an equal, uniform register. Aspects of human life and personality are presented, copied, and distributed as if existence were confined to an endless tableau of clashing thumbnails; the illusion is that we can see what we want of others—and when—and ignore the rest. This is not conversation, as many social media platforms would have it, but consumption—the spectatorship of each other, and thus deeply antisocial.

So too in the way COVID-19 was shown to us: those images of emptiness invited us to consume a disaster in isolation, our attention drawn not to the way these images might be related but to how they are individual, and thus unrelated. We were, as ever, offered a choice: How do *I* want to experience the novelty of a global pandemic?

Just as a highly contagious disease revealed our bodies to

be in some way connected—even if some of those bodies were in luxury apartments while others slept in housing projects or on sidewalks—it revealed the social limits of consumerist activity. Years spent collecting "experiences" with one another—fitness classes, drag brunches, bars and restaurants so loud that conversation is discouraged, escape rooms, viewing parties, and whatever else can be photographed and uploaded for later—have damaged our capacity for experiencing one another on nontransactional terms. Without the ability to spend money and call it "having fun," we found ourselves as empty, as abandoned, as the train stations and supermarket aisles drifting through our timelines.

"The element of contagion," Canetti goes on, "which plays so large a part in an epidemic, has the effect of making people separate from each other . . . It is strange to see how the hope of survival isolates them, each becoming a single individual confronting the crowd of victims." This is what we've come to see, even before the pandemic, in our social media feeds: individuals confronting the crowd, staking their hope on remaining apart, viewing one another as distant spectacles. Yet unlike the inner isolation fostered by consumerism, the isolation of quarantine became a physical—and highly visible—reality. Without our public spaces ("public" meaning, in that American way, private places where you can be among others as long as you spend money), it became easier than ever to see our conceptual, spiritual isolation—each of us a private and lonely last person on earth. Confronting the spectacle of others with little to no contact or shared transactional space burst the last illusory bubble that consuming others as images was ever social at all. As Americans, we saw, for perhaps the first time, the extent of what the fascist imagination had done to us.

***

One of surrealism's clichés is that it is "the art of the dream." It seems, now—not only after a pandemic, but after fascism moved from our consumptive habits into the streets (and into the White House)—as if a long dream has ended. Rather than being pushed into the surreal, we have been for the first time in decades dislodged from the surreal. We now have a crucial opportunity to confront and accept reality.

Here's another cliché. In 1927, Fred Barnard, a manager at Street Railways Advertising, placed an ad for his agency's services

CHINESE PROVERB
One picture is worth
ten thousand words

in *Printers' Ink*. Hiring a calligrapher, Barnard declared that "One picture is worth ten thousand words," beneath, presumably, this same phrase in logographic Chinese, as well as the assurance that this was a "CHINESE PROVERB." Barnard later admitted he made this up: there was no Chinese proverb (yet many continue to attribute the phrase to Confucius).

The intimation in Barnard's oft misquoted phrase—an image now devalued to *one* thousand words instead of ten—is that one picture can replace those words, just as a single Euro, as I write this, can replace approximately $1.20. But the currency of words is more fluid than the cliché assumes. Each word, itself an abstraction, is an image in and of itself tangled up with other words: they're not so easily traded as commodities. Even in Barnard's ad, it's this connection of the words to the image above them that gives the image its meaning: they are the caption that articulates the action the image demands. Without its caption, Barnard's proverb has no language—and no politics.

Incidentally, Barnard's Chinese could translate closer to "One's picture's meaning can express ten thousand words." Worth, itself so American, had already slipped out of the picture.

A caption does not explain its image, nor interpret it. These are not two currencies—a picture and some verbal change—presented side by side. What a caption provides is context. It situates the picture, often in a place and time, but also as a politics—it teaches us how to read the image, which is mute without it. Literally "with text," context is the with-ness that clarifies an image's speech. This is what the light we've been given shows us: the space between an image and its speech, between *this* and *that* or *us* and *them*.

Once the relationships between images, between words, and between people are erased, they become vulnerable to manipulation. Once human beings or historical events become aestheticized as separate, out-of-time concepts—when the September 11 attacks, for example, are reduced to a tragedy that we must never forget, or when the government declares war against a contagious and deadly virus—someone or a group of someones is manipulating sentiment in order to profit, whether by dollar or by death. The costs of this, as we've seen in the United States and in Europe—not to mention all the countries vulnerable to American and European politics—have been enormous and will mount exponentially.

If there is a central question in this book, it is this: Who gets to police how we see ourselves and others? How much authority over our expression, as well as our perceptions of those around us, do we surrender to peers, elders, social media, art, entertainment, corporations, and the covers of magazines? If there is a central cost, it is everything: not only literal human lives, as we've seen in a deadly yet preventable pandemic as well as the resurgence of strict image-regimes like white nationalism and male chauvinism in mainstream political discourse, but—as a largely unchallenged allegiance to profit over planet continues to destroy our world's ability to sustain human life—the future of our species.

An ignorance of the ethics and politics of image consumption has brought about a time of such shattering trauma that it's almost incomprehensible. This trauma is borne of grief: as a culture, as a society, and as individuals across the planet, we have suffered immense personal and collective losses, including the possible loss of the future itself.

But that word, possible, contains a hope. The destruction of our ecosphere is not inevitable, nor is a reductive subservience to harmful ideologies that make a handful of people richer at the expense of all of humanity. These structures are not small, nor easily untangled, but they are easily challenged; and it is the ethical imperative of every single person on earth to challenge them. To thrive, or even survive, we must find a life beyond the fascist imagination—a life where it's not only possible, but easy to imagine confronting a global disaster, be it a pandemic or something far larger and more gradually insidious, without the temptation to monetize it, entertain oneself with it, surrender to it, or hang one's personality on its hook.

Everyone has the right to that life. Everyone has the right to resist. In *Zvizdal [Chernobyl, so far—so close]*, a "cinematic play" and documentary about the lives of an elderly couple who farmed in solitude for decades within the Ukraine's Exclusion Zone, Nadia Lubenoc goes to fetch a bucket of water from a well. Over the years, she's developed a strong limp, and moves slowly across the field. What happens, her interviewer wants to know, when she can no longer bear the weight? "If you can't carry a bucket," she replies, "then carry a cup."

As long as we live, we are free to narrate an anti-fascist future. Next to nothing, a cup is enough.

I

WHAT A TIME TO CALL THIS ALIVE

The president's daughter was unhappy. Just after dawn on the fourth of April, 2017, Syrian warplanes launched missiles armed with sarin gas at residential areas in Khan Shaykhun, killing 92 and injuring over 500, including medical personnel and rescue workers. There were no armories, airbases, or rebels in the area: "just people," according to one doctor. After the attack, reported *Syria Direct*, many residents "refused to believe their relatives were dead, and are currently holding on to their bodies in the hopes that they will wake up." Sarin is a nerve agent that brings asphyxiation by paralysis; victims are no longer able to control the muscles that enable them to breathe. In one photograph, boys as young as four or five lie in a tangle of pale, rigid limbs. In another, a young man holds two grey infants in his arms, their cheeks the color of bruises. On Facebook and Twitter, these photographs appeared in between jokes, sponsored ads for fast food and dating apps, and the latest interpretation of whatever it was the president himself had defamed that morning.

Heartbroken, actually, was the word Ivanka Trump had used. "Heartbroken and outraged," she tweeted, "by the images coming out of Syria following the atrocious chemical attack yesterday." Her father, until then aloof, decided to launch fifty-nine Tomahawk cruise missiles at the Shayrat airbase, from which the chemical attack was thought to originate. In an interview with *The Telegraph*, Eric Trump speculated that his sister's heartbreak held sway over their father's decision to retaliate: "Ivanka is a mother of three kids and she has influence. I'm sure she said: 'Listen, this is horrible stuff.' My father will act in times like that." Presumably, she showed her father the images of dead children well after he knew that children had died. In a statement at his Florida mansion, Trump acknowledged that "Even beautiful babies were cruelly murdered in this very barbaric attack. No child of God should ever suffer such horror." Newspapers hailed his speech as "presidential." Even long-term critics of the administration praised his decision, at last, to bomb another country. He had overcome his incompetence and pettiness, they implied, and become a true leader.

The missiles failed to disable the airbase. The following week, in an interview with *Fox Business*, Trump had forgotten which country he'd attacked. A few days later, he dropped the most powerful weapon any nation has used against another in over seventy years. The target was a small district of Afghanistan, home to ninety-five thousand men, women, and children. That same month, *The New York Times* reported that eighteen Syrian rebels had been killed in the latest U.S. air strike, which was "the third time in a month that American-led air strikes may have killed civilians or allies." There were no images of these civilians, of these children, and no word of heartbreak.

These are not new concerns, even in Syria. Nearly a year after the Khan Shaykhun attack, critic Michael Kimmelman observed how *The New York Times* had published four separate but eerily similar photographs. Each was taken after an air strike in January or February of 2018 in eastern Ghouta, a suburb of Damascus. Each foregrounds an adult carrying a child, usually bloodied, against a monochrome backdrop of smoke, rubble, and dust. "At one time," Kimmelman writes, "images of Syria galvanized our attention."

But now, one city looks like another, one neighborhood—even one child—like another. "Photographs of fractured silhouettes of bombed-out buildings blend together. This leveling is Mr. Assad's triumph." That each new photograph from Syria looks familiar undercuts their power: "Syrian photographers have produced some remarkable images. But novel photographs in the midst of brutal airstrikes are not easy to make." Even the novelty of the war selfie, with which many Syrians "have tried to reach out on their own, circulating videos on social media of their pleading children," has become ubiquitous and, ultimately, overlooked. It's a similar numbness, a similar leveling, that invites Americans, informed every day or so that the president has committed another unconstitutional or treasonous act, to shrug our shoulders.

By now, one has come to expect images of pain, suffering, shock, and horror in the daily (or hourly) consumption of the news, at home and abroad. Syria itself, like Bosnia, like Palestine, like Flint, like Ferguson, has become an image—a metonym for an ongoing disaster no one seems moved to stop. These are situations that Ariella Azoulay, in *The Civil Contract of Photography*, calls "on the verge of catastrophe." Living conditions in these areas would normally require a state of emergency; this is how fully recognized citizens in wealthy countries respond to such things as "terror attacks." But in areas of the world—including areas within wealthy countries—that delineate fully recognized citizens from noncitizens or vulnerable citizens, these conditions can be so prolonged and ongoing that there is no recognition of disaster. This creates, Azoulay writes, "a paradoxical situation in which the injury to the population of noncitizens is simultaneously visible and invisible." There is no event to observe or repair, and no clear demarcation in time anyone can point to that offers a desired normalcy.

Unlike Steve Liss's photograph of the fence where Matthew Shepard was left to die, there is no single photograph of Syria that claims to speak. There is no photograph of a young girl, her face frozen in horror, as napalm sears the skin from her body. Instead, with its ongoingness, "Syria" evokes not just outrage and heartbreak but resignation: nothing has been done; nothing will be done. In the United States, the next time a video surfaces of our own country's no-trial, state-sponsored murders, there will be outrage. There will be heartbreak. There may even be riots. But above all there will be resignation: *we*, as a nation, have already seen hundreds of images like these, and white police officers continue to murder Black citizens with impunity.

That photographs of dead children are horrific but not unfathomable—that one can anticipate and bear their faces in the morning paper or in the glow of some workplace computer screen—is a failure of our civic responsibility toward one another as human beings. This is what Azoulay means by "the civil contract of photography"—an obligation not only to look passively at photographs but to *watch* them. She riffs on Roland Barthes's notion of the photograph as a testimony of what "was there" and rebels against the idea that photographs offer moments of time frozen or time stopped: "The verb 'to watch' is usually used for regarding phenomena or moving pictures. It entails dimensions of time and movement that need to be reinscribed in the interpretation of the still photographic image."

Free idea: A series of gifs or short videos that start as still re-creations of famous images depicting suffering, and that come to life and into full color as they continue—the girl in Vietnam screaming as she burns, the soldier in Spain falling to the grass amid gunfire and smoke, and many more.

Human beings do not exist frozen in time but fluid in time; we are time's contemporaries. Images of people in pain mean there are, or were, people who experienced—and may be out there experiencing as we watch the photograph—such pain. To watch photographs brings them out of the past, where nothing can be done, and into the present, where the past is a map, something to guide us onward. To imagine photographs in motion is not to clip them from our lives and cement them in the past but to include them alongside us, in our own movement toward a shared future. One has to believe we invented silver gelatin, and later celluloid, to bring the past with us, not leave it behind.

Conversely, to look at photographs as documents of what "was there" is to abandon one's responsibility toward other human beings. It is to sympathize, as Sontag writes, rather than act: "These sights carry a double message. They show a suffering that is outrageous, unjust, and should be repaired. They confirm that this is the sort of thing which happens in that place. The ubiquity of those photographs, and those horrors, cannot help but nourish belief in the inevitability of tragedy in the benighted or backward—that is, poor—parts of the world." In Syria, as these photographs can be made to say, children occasionally asphyxiate from inhaling lethal substances launched by their own governments. In low-income neighborhoods throughout America, as uploaded videos can be made to say, Black Americans are gunned down or strangled, their murderers unpunished.

Perhaps, then, these photographs aren't being made to say enough? "We mourn when a single whale gets caught in a net and dies," Kimmelman writes, "but throw up our hands at climate change. The scale of suffering in a place like Ghouta seems almost too big and painful to grasp . . . There's an argument that coarsened culture requires even more gruesome photographs to rouse our numbed humanity." It was, after all, the images of "beautiful babies," presumably, that changed the president's mind. At least if one overlooks the greater politics of Trump's and Putin's respective presidencies, both of which intersect in Syria.

Vladimir Putin is an unashamed and fervent supporter of Assad's regime and concurrent mass murder. Trump has, repeatedly, boasted of his admiration for Putin despite repeated reports from multiple intelligence agencies that indicate Putin's interference in U.S. elections and legislative policy, as well as in those of our European allies. In that same *Telegraph* interview, Eric Trump called his father's retaliation "proof" that the family is not allied with Putin, even though the counterattack did nothing to disable Assad's military capabilities. Cynically, I could say that the president's fifty-nine missiles were nothing but fireworks. They did, after all, earn him that long-sought moniker, presidential, even if only for a few days. He did get to say, "No child of God should ever suffer such horror" in front of the cameras, despite everything he's done to children and their families since, including separate them, attack them with tear gas, and allow them to suffer abuse and to die from neglect or coronavirus in concentration camps along the southern border.

The image of an American president is one who bombs, mournfully, people who aren't white, and for a brief moment the image of Trump and the image of an American president coincided, a relief many had been waiting for ever since the anxiety itself—"president-elect Donald Trump"—was created.

But what would children have to look like, in the next photographs? Under what circumstances must we see them suffering in order to say, *Something must be done*, rather than *It's terrible how things are* while we shrug and turn away? What will we demand of a photograph the next time it purports to mean something, to teach us something? As Teju Cole observes, "A photograph cannot show human rights, but it can depict, with terrifying realism, what a starving person looks like, what a human body looks like after it has been shot." In this syntax, the hope is that terror—or terrifying realism—will do something. This is a faith our culture has long placed in photographs, particularly those of war and of suffering: if we see it, and viscerally, we will no longer tolerate it. It's a faith placed entirely in aesthetics, in the idea that something can appear so perfectly terrible that we, as viewers, will be overwhelmed and change our lives. Like any aesthetics, there is no finality to this, there is no "enough." The history of art is a history of metamorphosis, of saying the same thing in new and unfamiliar ways; to focus on the aesthetics of an image, on how it says "children are suffering," is to search for new ways to delight, however terribly, in such pain.

In 1985, Frances Lindley Fralin assembled *The Indelible Image: Photographs of War—1846 to the Present* for the Grey Gallery in New York. She hoped, she said, "to make a statement about the absurdity and futility of war." Even images from the nineteenth century rarely shy away from death, despite their embrace of the mundane. Not only do soldiers gather to exercise or to organize their weapons or to line up in a field; so too do they clean up battlefields, pile corpses, and corral hostages. Reviewing the exhibition for *The Village Voice*, Gary Indiana noted its sly intention. Despite the obvious—that "war is not only absurd and futile, but sad, lethal, and extremely photogenic"—there is a cumulative anesthetization; the images themselves begin to mean nothing. Instead, like individual words strung together, they form a larger argument, or even a story: "The image of the photographer, snapping away as the world burns, begins to supplant the pictures before one's eyes . . . On the imaginative level, the generous visceral grossness of 'The Indelible Image' melts away, in many instances, into an appreciation of war photography as narrative fiction." Once the photographer's gaze becomes visible within one's own, we read the photograph as we would an authorial construct: so-and-so saw this, just as I am writing this. The viewer isn't seeing war for oneself, but being shown another's vision of war. "In these photographs," Indiana concludes, "reality has become a fiction, the fiction of objectivity: lower the camera to the floor level, change the lighting, and you've got a whole different kind of truth on your hands."

Photographs don't speak; they are used as speech. Photographs don't mean; they are imbued with meaning. "The kinds of details photographs are good at are visual and affective," Cole writes, "different from the kinds of details we might call 'political,' which have to do with laws, fine shades of linguistic meaning and the distribution of power." To infer meaning from the visual, from the affective, is to place an inordinate trust, or even hope, in photography: if we become afraid enough, moved enough, the photograph will have said, definitively, that suffering exists and must be stopped. It will have told us what to do and how to do it. The hope for any photograph of suffering or atrocity is to show us the *last* photograph of suffering or atrocity that humankind will ever have to see. Strangely, no such photographs exist. There are no last photographs of suffering or atrocity—only of individual human beings, of creatures, of places. The last photograph of a northern white rhino, the last photograph of the Hetch Hetchy Valley, the last photograph of George Floyd or Matthew Shepard or a toddler in Syria; these subjects existed, but no longer. Meanwhile suffering is immortal, atrocity ever resurrected.

***

There's something Christian in the photograph of the fence where Matthew Shepard was found dying, with no small influence from the murder's apocrypha. *Vanity Fair* noted that he'd been "crucified," even though his hands, according to the police report, were tied behind his back. The tear tracks one imagines on his face—visible only, said the officer who untied him, because they'd washed away his blood—imbue his suffering with resignation rather than fear, with sorrow for having lived in such a world rather than anger or panic at having to leave it. There are the facts: he was five two and 105 pounds, blond, boyish, and wore braces. Yet none of these, the facts or the stories, are present in Steve Liss's photograph itself; there is only the fence, at dawn, embracing the first glow of sun as it looms over the ground, which remains in shadow. The posts themselves, mottled and rough, seem primal and hastily constructed. From one of them, someone has hung a basket of flowers whose petals weep or drip over the side. Even the X of each support post is asymmetrical; they all have the look of leaning crosses, one after another toward the horizon.

Despite its ubiquity in images, suffering is not a subject; it is an aesthetic. Viewing or imagining human beings in pain, often in decontextualized situations, is a visual solicitation of emotions. That reporters eagerly indulged certain details surrounding Shepard's murder, such as the tracks tears had made on his face, or his height and weight, and omitted others, such as his alleged addiction to and distribution of crystal meth or his prior acquaintance with one of his murderers, betrays their aestheticization of an event: his death cut from reality like a clipping from a newspaper and pasted on the board of hate crimes. They focused on his suffering in the same register as that of James Byrd Jr., earlier that same year, who was beaten and tortured by three white men, chained to a pickup truck, and dragged for three miles along an asphalt road. Paraphrasing the Reverend Jesse Jackson, *The New York Times* reported that Byrd "had entered the pantheon of the nation's racial martyrs and victims," and suggested "a monument in his memory as a tangible protest against hate crimes." Today, the James Byrd Jr. Memorial Park in Jasper, Texas, has 4.2 out of 5 stars on Google Maps. One reviewer has uploaded photos to document that "Charlee"—a young girl smiling on a swing set—"had a blast!"

Remembered properly, murders like these become atrocities. Like those killed at Columbine High School in April of 1999, or the victims of the 2001 attacks on the World Trade Center, they "enter the pantheon" of *prescriptive memory*, where we, as a nation, are taught to remember such violence as historical, as part of our education. And thus we are educated. We build the memorials. We "never forget" Shepard, Byrd, Columbine, 9/11. We promise: "Never Again." Usually, similar if not eerily identical circumstances crop up again, with new victims and, ultimately, new memorials. Suffering is among the most instructive of forms, with a syllabus increasingly contemporary.

"Never Again," as a slogan, has changed over the decades. Now hashtagged to nearly any protest against violence, the phrase originally referred to the Nazi genocide against Jews. As Emily Burack writes in *The Jerusalem Post*, "The phrase gained currency in English thanks in large part to Meir Kahane, the militant rabbi who popularized it in America when he created the Jewish Defense League in 1968." Gradually, a sense of remembrance and a desire for peace eclipsed Kahane's militancy. "Never Again," Burack writes, "is a phrase that keeps on evolving. It was used in protests against the Muslim ban and in support of refugees, in remembrance of Japanese internment during World War II and recalling the Chinese Exclusion Act of 1882."

In truth, Liss's photograph is beautiful, and meant to be. The 9/11 Memorial in Lower Manhattan—with its two black pools emptying into the foundations of the towers, the names of victims lining the railings of both fountains—is beautiful. In Chile, at the Museo de la Memoria y los Derechos Humanos, there is a fifty-foot-high wall covered in 3,197 photographs, all faces of Chileans murdered under Augusto Pinochet's seventeen-year dictatorship. In Montgomery, Alabama, the National Memorial for Peace and Justice contains "more than 800 stele-like, 6-foot-tall rusted steel mini-monuments," as critic Holland Cotter describes them. Each is inscribed with the name of a county, as well as with a list of the names of African Americans (sometimes "Unknown") who were lynched there. As the walking path gradually descends, these coffin-like structures, which initially surround viewers, are soon suspended overhead, suggesting bodies hanging from trees, and "so high that the inscribed names are unreadable."

What all of these memorials do—and do well—is engage the senses. In size, in starkness, in beauty, in contrast of color or shadow, and in their mass deployment of names or faces, they overwhelm the eye. They offer an emotional experience that betrays what they really are: art. That is, they are not straightforward records of events as they happened, but stylized interpretations or translations. As art, they must be approached, discussed, and critiqued as objects or images with artistic intent: *Who created this, and what do they want me to feel or to think?* They must not be studied, and certainly not revered, as history.

Like photographs, memorials aestheticize suffering and atrocity. With their unique names and executions, each adapts a real-life event into a complete story; often, we call them tragedies. Commemorating tragedies we cannot change, populated by people we cannot save, memorials invite us to regard the fixed and motionless past from our mercurial present. Prescriptive memory, then, composed of curated atrocities, becomes a gallery instead of a sequence of related events: a canon of terrible images we're supposed to understand simply by looking at them.

In any society, this gallery of pain highlights its obsessions, concerns, and fears. If one examines the way American society curates and archives its atrocities, one begins to understand the nation's self-serving relationship to history, where the aestheticization of atrocity not only seems like a useless deterrent against violence, but actually to justify it, to encourage it.

In a 1995 interview, discussing the Serbian slaughter of Bosnians, Sontag remarked on the lack of action from other European nations, all signatories to the Convention on the Prevention and Punishment of the Crime of Genocide: "'Never again' doesn't mean anything, does it? I mean, never again will Germans be allowed to kill Jews in the 1940s, that's true." Despite the phrase's apparent universality, when it comes to its application, Sontag is right: Because we refuse to recognize atrocities for what they are, "Never Again" doesn't stray far from its original connotation. Unfortunately, building memorials and planting gardens and reciting names is never enough. It's not only ineffective but unethical to outsource our political engagement with history to commemorative beauty, to substitute thinking about real events with being moved by mere works of art. If art could speak the way we pretend it does, there would be no "again" at all.

This is, however, why art is taught. Despite the claims of several artists and writers throughout the centuries—nearly all in positions of immense privilege and power—artworks are more than aesthetic. This is what contemporary cancel culture is clumsily trying to untangle—that artworks have ethics, and that engaging, buying, and sharing art has ethical obligations. Cancel culture is not censorship but a protest against systemic injustice, against aesthetic supremacy—the lie that beauty trumps all in cinema, photographs, literature, and so on. It is anti-fascism as criticism, and once it maps the ethical and political obligations in its own language and tactics, it will address injustices in the arts, both historical and contemporary, on par with the greatest discursive movements against power—including feminism, Marxism, queer theory, and intersectionality—in critical history.

***

Americans, generally, aren't so good at history. It's tempting to think our propensity for dramatizing wars, disasters, and other so-called tragedies onstage and in cinema has been detrimental to our understanding of events, populating collective memory with individual stories, as if episodes from an epic. In episodic narratives, nothing ever changes—everything is normal in the beginning, terrible in the middle, and resolved by the end. Characters and settings are comfortably static. With respect to real-life atrocity, this is how the United States has lost its innocence at least half a dozen times, from the Civil War to 9/11 to Trump's election. Everything that happens is a shock to the nation. This is how our never again becomes ever again: an innocence déjà perdu.

History, after all, is heavy. For many Americans, it's something to leave behind. We say we're post-race; we say same-sex marriage put an end to homophobia. To do this we tell stories of slavery and civil rights,

In a 1975 interview, Sontag quipped that the American relationship with history was one of disinterest, even fear: "The essential American relation to the past is not to carry too much of it. The past impedes action, saps energy. It's a burden because it modifies or contradicts optimism . . . You take a photograph before you destroy something. The photograph is its posthumous existence."

of the AIDS epidemic. These are photos we snap and label as past. Indeed, history itself is something our nation, as an idea, tried to escape—the entrenchments of Europe, the legacies of kings, and whatever else the wealthy white men who created our country on paper promised themselves.

In truth, we are history; our unique pasts exist only in the present. In forsaking them for prescriptive memory, particularly without interrogating who has prescribed us these memories, we place a tenuous hope in what writer and psychotherapist Adam Phillips calls "a redemptive myth." We believe, he says in "The Forgetting Museum," that "remembering done properly will give us the lives that we want." In saying, *Look what happened*, there is an optimism that the image itself will carry the pain and do the work, all in a gamble that atrocity will look the same when and if it reappears. That, ultimately, is prescriptive memory's weakness; even two real, literal photographs taken of the same person are never identical. To rely upon images instead of contextualized history is to guarantee getting lost.

Not that we're always meant to find our way. Some memorials, for example, are particularly careful images of the past. Their aesthetics harbors a desired emotional, not intellectual, understanding: Viewers and visitors are meant to feel, not think. At the 9/11 Memorial and Museum, the aesthetics of absence—two seemingly bottomless black pools surrounded by the names of the thousands who died—alongside recovered detritus, burned clothing, rubble, and the final voicemails of those trapped inside, all frame a narrative of destruction that points to a strangely opaque other: al-Qaeda. Absent altogether is Osama bin Laden's long relationship with the United States government. To contextualize him among the names, faces, and voices of the dead—especially as a CIA-funded militant in the Soviet–Afghan War—would politicize something more easily remembered as tragedy. Yet there was nothing apolitical about the destruction of the World Trade Center, and to expunge politics from the memorial is its own political act, the effect of which is to stir grief, incite rage, and mobilize Americans against an ambiguous enemy. As I write this, what is still branded "the War on Terror" has surpassed its nineteenth year, its sixth trillionth dollar, and the end of anywhere between half a million and two million lives. Demanding that we never forget is laughable if, from the start, there's no genuine history to remember; and "Never Again" means nothing when victims are aestheticized as propaganda, when our own government uses them to amplify retributive terror.

***

Americans are also bad at propaganda—that is, at recognizing it. As producers and consumers of propaganda, the United States outperforms every other nation in the world. For most of us, the word connotes negatively. It's the odor to advertising's scent, a reputation created by propaganda of our own: the way propaganda is portrayed, for example, in history and in fictions of the U.S.S.R. and the Third Reich, not to mention countless dystopian futures imagined by authors and filmmakers. But propaganda, as Andrew O'Hagan wrote for *T* magazine a few months after the 2016 elections, does not necessarily come from one man in power who "supplant[s] what is true with what they wish to be true." Instead, propaganda stems from "an impulse to choose a side and press its case with wily elegance," and what it "sells" is a way of life, or "a series of values, traits and skills that others might do well to emulate." O'Hagan's words are precise—"might do well to emulate"— and reflect how propaganda excels. It doesn't demand or dictate so much as suggest, aggressively. "Manipulating human belief might sound like an alarming project for governments and designers to undertake," he adds, but

> it's one of the oldest professions in the book, and corporations, religions, entertainers and doctors, to say little of politicians, are dedicated to the art of making you think what you ought to think. Populism is based on the notion that people can think for themselves, but most people can't and don't want to; they need team colors and a direction of play that is worked out by other people . . . For good or for ill, the art of propaganda must set out to persuade them of what they think.

Indeed, it's this "for good" that has been most overlooked in the United States, even though we see good propaganda at work every day, and have for decades—in certain commercials, for example, when nearly every race and gender and sexual orientation is equally represented in its consumption, say, of heartburn medication; or in film after film where money, no matter how hard the rich man tries, can't bring him what he wants, not even happiness.

It was a little more obvious, O'Hagan notes, during World War II, when it was "considered by most of the Allies to be something of a gentle and spirited approach to the survival of the species." In 1943, the United States Department of War produced a short film called *Don't Be a Sucker*. The film features one-dimensional Americans going about their lives, yet reminds us that this is a country full of "free people" of many different religions who go to their own churches and form their own opinions. But, the film's narrator says, "There are guys who stay up nights figuring out how to take that away." The film cuts to a middle-aged man, sour with anger as he preaches from the steps of a government building. "I'm just an average American," this man says, "but I'm an *American* American . . . I see Negroes holding jobs that belong to me and you." He rants about what must be done, who must stick together and who must be excluded, while two men in the audience debate his speech. "He seems to know what he's talking about," the younger of the two says, but his perception is quickly dismantled by the older man, whose Hungarian accent connotes an authority on "what this talk can do." In America, he says, "we have no *other* people. We are American people." He informs the younger man how the Nazis came to power, how their rhetoric divided the populace. "We human beings are not born with prejudices," he says. "Always they are made for us. Made by someone who wants something. Remember that when you hear this kind of talk. Somebody is going to get something out of it. And it isn't going to be you." The film is a brilliant piece of anti-fascist, pro-American propaganda, appealing not to the sympathies of others but to the young man's self-interests: the focus is not on the fate of minorities in fascism's crosshairs, but on how fascism won't bring prosperity to the young man, only those using him as a pawn.

After the War, however, American propaganda began to differentiate itself from state-driven efforts in countries designated as political enemies—an executive strategy seen as incompatible with the freedom of the individual. O'Hagan cites the CIA's famous covert literary magazine, *Encounter*, as one example to "win the hearts and minds of the English-speaking world," as well as Hollywood's decades-long project to "churn out pro-war propaganda and sexist assumptions as if they were catnip to the people." Whether funded by the government or not, these corporate propaganda systems reinforce the image of the United States the government has established, which in turn benefits wealthy donors and lobbyists whose funding influences legislation that complements this propaganda.

During the Trump presidency, state-driven propaganda returned to the limelight, complete with slogans, an emphasis on loyalty, a racially based isolation of who is elevated as American and who is not, and a flagrant disregard for what is true in place of what one man in power wishes to be true. In fact, the phenomenon of Donald Trump embodies not only how propaganda functions in this country today, but how an image's politics depends entirely upon context. Not only does one see the tenuous, even fragile relationship between images and language, there is an increasing acquaintance with the relationship of images with other images, whose juxtapositions become a language in and of themselves. I'm thinking of Hillary Clinton's 2016 campaign ad, in which the iridescently lit faces of children filled the screen while actual footage of Donald Trump played out on the televisions they were presumably watching. "What will our children think?"

Lest we forget, the president made 2,140 *observable* false or misleading claims in his first year of office, or 5.9 lies per day.

Clinton's voice-over asks while Trump degrades immigrants and women and Muslims and persons with disabilities to enthusiastic cheers. It was a beautiful and earned work of propaganda, giving context to an image (Trump) by placing it against another (children, shorthand for America's future). But so too was the president's lexicon of epithets ("Crooked Hillary" Clinton, "Lyin' Ted" Cruz) a successful deployment of propaganda, and so too his talent for slogans. Above all—by focusing on crime in border states, Islamic terrorism, the legitimacy of President Obama's birth, and "urban" violence—it was his aggressive suggestion that whiteness in America was under attack that proved most successful among a vicious and victorious minority of voters. Through propaganda, Trump overtly politicized whiteness in a way Americans had not seen in a presidential election since George Wallace's pro-segregation campaign in 1968. Unlike Wallace, he won. This didn't come out of nowhere. We've been learning to see "fascistly" for decades; it's only now that our government reflects it so brazenly.

***

While details in images may not be political, images themselves, especially images of combat, suffering, and violence—images that aestheticize atrocity—are explicitly political. Images of war, especially those brought before "uninvolved" third parties, are meant to defend or demean those whose homes war has visited, whose streets war has walked. They are meant to solicit allegiance, be it to peace or to genocide. Identically political are photographs of poverty and sickness, such as Alec Soth's portraits of opioid-addicted mothers and their children for *The New York Times Magazine* in May 2018. Soth's photographs say what all photographs of persons struggling with opioid addiction published in mainstream magazines and newspapers say: namely, these drugs aren't just killing anyone, they are killing white women and white children, and something must be done to stop it.

Photographs of children in pain or poverty or their death throes, as discussed above, are exclusively political, particularly for viewers in nations we

call developed. Kimmelman highlights this when discussing those four similar Syrian photographs by including a fifth: "a cherubic boy in a pink sweater, perched on the edge of a sofa, reaching toward a bright pink flower." The boy is Jad Allah Jumaa, and his picture, Kimmelman writes, is one "that loving parents all over the world take every day," but without its tragedy: "Maybe we need to stare at a simple, everyday family snapshot to remember what binds us. Like that one of Jad Allah Jumaa. He was 1-1/2 years old when he died on Feb. 21 in an air strike on eastern Ghouta. He was wearing his pink sweater." In this photo, we see the boy as we ought to see him—the socially conjured state in which one expects to encounter children: smiling, happy, camera-conscious, cared-for, alive.

Juxtaposed against the images of children from the Khan Shaykhun attack, Kimmelman's use of Jumaa's portrait acquires rhetoric: What kind of global politics allows children like these to die, and so terribly? How could we let this happen? It's this same "we" one belongs to when looking at Soth's photographs, at videos of Black men murdered by police, at the photograph of a woman with two children fleeing a cloud of tear gas just outside the U.S. border, and even in circulated images of the president's most minor actions—walking in front of his wife rather than beside her, for example, or leaving an umbrella on the ground for someone else to pick up. It's the "we" placed in front of all these images—the implication of shared responsibility—that gives each its politics, which in its very etymology predicates our mutual involvement. A politics is nothing without its *polis*, the assemblage of human beings it governs.

An implication of shared experience and responsibility, however, is not a plea for sympathy: it wants neither wishes nor apologies. What these photographs placed in these contexts ask of their viewers is not compassion but action. As Sontag observes, compassion can impede action:

> So far as we feel sympathy, we feel we are not accomplices to what caused the suffering. Our sympathy proclaims our innocence as well as our impotence. To that extent, it can be (for all our good intentions) an impertinent—if not an inappropriate—response. To set aside the sympathy we extend to others beset by war and murderous politics for a reflection on how our privileges are located on the same map as their suffering, and may—in ways we might prefer not to imagine—be linked to their suffering, as the wealth of some may imply the destitution of others, is a task for which the painful, stirring images supply only an initial spark.

Similar to how photographs of dead or injured children in Syria "confirm that this is the sort of thing which happens in that place," a sympathy with these children and their families reinforces the separation imagined between this place and that place, or more importantly, the distance between us and them. Sympathy impedes action when the "we" implied in a photograph becomes "they." Politics is overlooked when an image's subjects are

One sees this same grammar of sympathy in charity, which is not only a way of deflecting political responsibility, but of actively reinforcing the inequality and suffering politics can create. Charity is a powerful way to ensure "they" never become part of the giver's "we."

excluded—consciously or otherwise—from the viewer's "we." But the politics remains no matter who chooses to see it or ignore it. To see the "we" in every image is indeed to understand its politics, and therefore place oneself in a capacity for action—the "initial spark" that Sontag mentions. While fueled by aesthetic skill, the ignition of that spark is, ultimately, outside the capability of the photographer, videographer, uploader, publisher, or any other image-maker or -sharer. If all images are political, not all viewers see or choose to see their politics; and there is nothing the image or image-maker can do within the image to demand that the viewer see its politics. This remains the province of language, which the viewer or spectator must bring to the image. If a divisive and isolating way of seeing enables a harmful politics—if erasing the "we" in an image is an act of the fascist imagination—to bring one's compassion to an image and situate it within the world is the foundation of the anti-fascist imagination.

***

An aesthetics that isolates or erases politics is doomed to reinvent itself, to disguise itself, as cleverly and artfully as possible; remembering atrocity is reduced to form, to play. Just as it's a reader's duty to understand a text, it is our duty as witnesses—not the photographer's or the photograph's—to work through what we are seeing. It is unethical to expect photographs, or memorials, or images of any kind to do our prescriptive work. Instead, we must bring that work to the image, or watch it as a shared moment from our living present—something we can respond to, even change.

But so too can we pay closer attention, and even reward, those images that invite action. In 2017, Santiago's Museo de la Memoria y los Derechos Humanos curated "Secrets of State: The Declassified History of the Chilean Dictatorship," an exhibit that offered a selection from more than twenty-three thousand American intelligence documents pertaining to Chile, including phone transcripts between Nixon and Kissinger regarding the "threat" of Salvador Allende's socialist government, dossiers on how to destabilize the country, and reports from the Chilean military requesting U.S. assistance with a coup. This exhibit was on display in the same building as the faces of those 3,197 Chileans extrajudicially murdered by Pinochet's government, and offers a clear link between the two. Unlike most memorials, the exhibit shows its tragedy in full context—that is, in time among other events, alongside other persons.

Back in Montgomery, a few blocks from the National Memorial for Peace and Justice, the newly built Legacy Museum offers another form of context. Progress is not the narrative here, as the *Times*'s Cotter points out, but an attempt "to document and dramatize a continuing condition of race-based oppression, one that has changed form over time, but not substance." The pain remembered in the Legacy Museum is openly political, placing whiteness in context and inviting white visitors not to empathize, exactly— not to see themselves in the victim—but to recognize their own actions, their fears, in the historic oppressor. After all, it's not the victims of political violence who get to decide "never again"; it's those who have the power to oppress. When a memorial aestheticizes the pain of victims while eclipsing or othering the role of oppressors, viewers are unlikely to recognize their own complicity in ongoing systemic violence. Instead, we have only a finished picture, however gruesome, hung in the gallery of the past.

This is why challenging the narrative of an atrocity is so upsetting to those who deeply connect with its tragedy. This is why I began this book with a photograph that means something to me: tragedy can change, and we along with it.

Stephen Jimenez, a journalist initially hired by *The New York Times*, spent thirteen years investigating the complicated circumstances surrounding Matthew Shepard's murder, most of them without institutional support. One of his many claims was that Shepard not only knew one of his murderers, but had had sex with him several times before accepting that ride out of town. In addition, Jimenez asserts, both were part of Laramie's supply chain of crystal meth. These details, published in *The Book of Matt* in 2013, make the murder more complicated than Liss's and other journalists' evocation of an angelic martyr. Since the book's publication, Jimenez, who is gay, has been boycotted and labeled a homophobe by gay rights organizations. Meanwhile, his research has done little to alter the cultural image of Shepard as a "crucified" angel, targeted and killed by strangers solely because he was gay.

While Jimenez carelessly overlooks the likelihood that drugs *and* homophobia led to Shepard's murder—McKinney, after all, refused to acknowledge his sexuality publicly, and acted aggressively to those who threatened to out him—the book is a useful document in contesting the canonical narratives of tragedies, however we choose to memorialize them. It's not, in the end, very instructive to say "Never Again" to some abstracted and senseless hate crime when, in fact, Shepard was a human being who suffered from depression, who self-medicated with drugs, who struggled with self-harm, and whose community failed him as a gay man, as an addict, as a mentally ill individual. So too did this same community fail Aaron McKinney, whose circumstances were very similar to Shepard's. Sadly, work like Jimenez's opens Shepard up to hate all over again, as exemplified by Dennis Prager's review of the book in the *National Review*, where he uses its premise to surmise that "truth is subordinated to whatever it is the Left most cares about," and discredits advances in gay rights, including a claim that "the media fabricated the heterosexual [AIDS] epidemic in order to remove stigma from gay males and in order to garner support for more AIDS-research money." This is the kind of hateful response gay rights organizations knew would come if journalists looked too closely at the complications of Shepard's life and death, and why the memory of Shepard's murder hangs in the hall of hate crimes—even though it was never prosecuted as one.

To flatten these events into an unfathomable hate crime erases a more granular reality, in which drug addiction, homophobia, mental illness, rural poverty, HIV status, and the Laramie Police Department's admitted lack of attention to an ongoing meth problem all converged upon a young, vulnerable man. So too are responses like Prager's part of this reality, in which we try to protect ourselves with a legislative category of crimes that immediately *others* its perpetrators rather than understand them as belonging to our systemically bigoted society. Targeting hate through slogans and foundations and beautiful photographs does not promise "Never Again"; it promises only not to recognize that "again" when it returns.

In what is now called the Holocaust, more than six million Jews were bureaucratically murdered by an elected government. Toni Morrison's *Beloved* is dedicated to the "Sixty Million and more" lives lost to slavery. By refusing to acknowledge the AIDS crisis, America closed its eyes to tens of thousands of gay men who died in excruciating pain, often alone. In the single greatest act of terror in human history, the United States incinerated and irradiated two hundred thousand Japanese civilians. On October 6, 1998, a young gay man suffering from depression and drug addiction was tied to a fence and beaten with a .357 magnum until his brain was so damaged it could no longer keep him alive.

I was thirteen when this happened, and I laughed when other boys in my grade, the boys whose attention and esteem I craved, called Shepard a faggot who got what was coming to him. This is a shame I've carried since. For years, I couldn't see myself in Matthew Shepard because he was innocently "out" and I was criminally "in," and so deeply that I too called him a faggot, that I said casually, in front of an adult gay couple the following summer, that fags should be more careful about who they try to flirt with. It wasn't until I read Jimenez's book—a book I too was furious to learn existed—that I recognized myself not only in Shepard's self-destruction but in McKinney's closeted violence, his willingness to destroy that part of himself he didn't like because our culture saw it (and still sees it) as a sickness.

Remembering the dead, damaged, discarded, tortured, and targeted is more than an aesthetic act. Their lives are not sacredly apolitical. Just as human beings have our overlapping diversities, so too are our atrocities intersectional. It is ethical to see and understand the context of their pain, to recognize ourselves not only in the victims but in the perpetrators. Every atrocity, like every photograph, asks that we recognize an "us"—never a "them." To recognize ourselves, our actions, and above all our capabilities in atrocity is an anti-fascist act that brings us closer to "Never Again" than any aesthetics ever can, no matter how many people pay for the privilege to dutifully weep without any understanding of what they've lost, and will again. To see "them" means only more weeping.

✳✳✳

Here's another innocence lost: On the morning of November 9, 2016, the world felt politicized beyond any recognizable capacity. But that world and its politics were always there. Jameson Fitzpatrick articulates this strange alienation and guilt in "I Woke Up":

> Who I thought was handsome was political.
> I went to work at the university and everything was
> very obviously political, the department and the institution.
> All the cigarettes I smoked between classes were political,

where I threw them when I was through.

I was blond and it was political.

So was the difference between "blond" and "blonde."

Coffee too is political. What is worn is political. These are statements meant to sound absurd but whose absurdity is only possible in a world filled with people who intentionally politicize—through what is called debate, through what are called conversations—the ability of individual human beings to live their lives. It becomes political, after all, "when America killed another person, / who they were and what color and gender and who I am in relation." Calling for gun control after another mass shooting is political, and deriding this as politicizing tragedy is equally political. "An issue can be encrusted with so many layers of 'politicization,'" as Jennifer Szalai puts it, "that an appeal to an apolitical high ground ends up looking like mere posturing." What is *not* political about the possibility for a human being to murder another human being, not to mention the patterns of these murders?—the similarity in weapons (assault rifle), the similarity in the murderers' socioeconomic backgrounds (white males with documented histories of aggression toward women or minorities)?

"To 'become politicized,'" Szalai writes, "is to become politically aware; to 'politicize an issue' is to make it a matter of public concern and to demand change . . . For those who benefit from the way things are, a raised consciousness is a threat." The very idea of a high ground—that mythical space of moral untouchability—is a political fabrication. It's an assumption that abstaining from what is "debatable" is somehow truer to life, more genuine, as though people don't lose their lives every day to politicized concepts like race, gender, climate change, reproduction, gun ownership, healthcare, and so on. It's this high ground where the context that reveals politics is erased, where someone who is white can hide from how whiteness works in a racist society, where someone who is male can hide from how "friendliness" or "jokes" can seem threatening to someone who identifies otherwise.

"Someone called me faggot and it was political. / I called myself a faggot and it was political": Fitzpatrick's poem toys with the vulnerability of isolated words, and the folly in thinking that who says them and when is irrelevant to their meaning. This is precisely what the term "just politics" tries to do to politics itself—to isolate it as a concept, to say it belongs only to its theater of elections, campaigns, speeches, and televised debates—its industry—when in fact it belongs to everyone and in every part of everyone's life. "Just politics" is the aestheticization of politics itself. "A politicized issue is one that's still a matter of public debate," Szalai writes, but to insist otherwise—"to strip an issue of its political dimensions" and place it in the past—is "blithe dismissal or brute force." This is why, for me, the morning of November 9 felt so politicized: I had believed white supremacy to be indefensibly beyond debate. I could believe this, like millions of others, because I am white, because white supremacy "didn't affect me." It's the same thinking that led an acquaintance of mine to say, in 2015, that gay men were no longer an oppressed minority, not after it became legal for us to get married. How could a country that elected a Black president still be so vulnerable to white supremacy?

It's for this same reason, presumably, that a world could witness the murder of six million Jews, the faces of burned and murdered villagers in Vietnam, the genocides in Bosnia and Rwanda and Palestine, only to stand by and look at newer and newer photographs of murdered Syrian children—these rigid little corpses in the arms of their parents—and say, *How terrible, something should be done*, knowing nothing will be done. This is just the sort of thing that happens in such a place. More importantly, this is the sort of thing that happens to such people—to people who aren't white. To erase this politics from every image of suffering is to pronounce a sentence of ongoing suffering, of endless images that aestheticize a decontextualized pain.

The failure to act, in looking at images, is a failure of ethics. Viewers deny themselves the context of these images: we see that these children and their families are not with us. We see that these images are not with other images. One word, even, is not with another. And just as images without other images or words without other words have no politics, the idea of "just politics"—an intellectual game of candidates and rhetoric—is possible only in isolation. A politics is predicated on being alongside other people and seeing them, understanding them, as people there with you; and we, more than any time in history, are unquestionably here together. Our actions and lack thereof affect one another more deeply than ever. Like images and like language, persons do not exist in isolation. We are all each other's context, situating one another on axes of place and of time, and it is our ethical responsibility not only to look but to watch each other, to offer our sincerest understandings, and to see what we truly are: us.

ere's another photograph from the cover of *Time*: Donald Trump hunched forward in a Louis XV lounge chair, moth-eaten, worn, half in shadow. His characteristic scowl, navy suit, and ostentatious tie complement the backdrop's gradient of midnight and slate, its mood, and *Time*'s shade of tarnished red. It's December of 2016 and Trump, the headline announces, is "Person of the Year"—the understatement of the decade. Despite this picture's similarities—the chair, the shadows, the scowl, the combovers—to the same magazine's portrait of Adolf Hitler in April 1941, what I'd really like to discuss is its frame.

All frames contextualize what they hold: oil paintings, vacation photos, pornography, advertisements, diplomas. A frame cleaves something from the rest of the world and says, *Contemplate this.* The frame of the image above—an American media institution that seems aware of the president-elect's cruelty, yet vulnerable to his celebrity—is an admission: this is the next president, and we must look at him. And a confession: we want to look at him. Indeed, for several years, it's felt as if he is all we can see.

Sometimes, frames take precedence. What media refer to as "content" is not only contextualized but determined by its frame. Content connotes a void in need of filling, the frame seeking an excuse to exist. Magazines, for example, that openly seek content (as opposed to essays, articles, stories, etc.) tell us as much about their own emptiness as they do about their perception of the culture at large. In a perverse poetics, a great majority of contemporary publishing creates a dynamic where the content of essays and articles is often borne of form—individual frames of links, banners, or advertisements. Online, where many of these ads blink, shift, or otherwise animate themselves, it's even clearer what it is we're actually supposed to contemplate.

Despite the internet, this is not a new development. As soon as newspapers began to augment subscription revenues with advertising, and thus seduce subscribers with lower prices, the frame of "newsworthy" began to shape what was considered news. This model is now standard, and even more effective when it comes to editorial content; hence the neoliberal, profit-driven ideology that most major media organizations tend to reflect. What this image + frame dyad did not anticipate, however—although it should have, given television's hypertrophic mutation and acceleration of advertising—was the dynamic of social media.

Nearly two years after the *Time* cover, the president himself posted a similar photograph: the same suit and tie, the same scowl, even the same background colors. This, however, was captioned "Sanctions are coming"—ostensibly in reference to the administration's foreign policy, but simultaneously a nod to *Game of Thrones*, a television series populated with political leaders who assassinate, torture, rape, castrate, imprison, mutilate, and humiliate their opponents—all to great fanfare. The stunt itself generated tens of thousands of words of reactionary content, be it praise, condemnation, or confusion, all of which brought users to familiar interfaces: blocks of text surrounded by advertisements, as well as an implicit invitation to comment on these texts, in case you'd like to return to the article later and see new advertisements.

A 2018 marketing email from Twitter, Inc., offered advice on engaging an audience: "Nothing moves faster than Twitter and it can be hard to come up with enough content ideas to keep up. But not every Tweet needs to be a masterpiece. In fact, it's much better to break dense pieces of content up into threads, sneak peaks [sic], and cross-promotions to stretch your updates over longer periods of time and have something to say each day." Twitter then suggests different ways of photographing your product, if applicable; ideas for public polls that invite agreement or disagreement with your opinions, should you have any; and tips for spreading awareness of your brand, whatever it may be.

Unlike a magazine or newspaper, Twitter doesn't care what your product or brand or worldview is. Users and advertisers are paired not by editorial design but by algorithmic calculation. Exempt from editorial responsibility, Twitter echoes the downfall of television and cable networks, pursuing inexpensive content—such as reality TV or nonstop political punditry—with maximum exposure. With more than 85 percent of the company's revenue (a little over $2.5 billion total in 2016) coming from advertising, it's easy to see how its mission—to "Give everyone the power to create and share ideas and information instantly, without barriers"—is subverted by the same "freedom" that preys on democracy itself: to maximize profit.

The pursuit of profit is always a race to the bottom. Despite 11 percent growth of "daily active usage" in 2016, Twitter became decreasingly attractive to advertisers. This shift began in the last quarter of that year, when @realDonaldTrump went from sensational curiosity to president-elect. A company executive defended its increasingly politicized traffic: "Having the political leaders of the world as well as news agencies participating on Twitter is an important part of reinforcing [engagement]." According to Twitter's terms of use, @realDonaldTrump should have been suspended years ago for his repeated incitements of violence and abuse of other users (rather than as late as 2021, when the insurrection at the Capitol removed any plausible deniability, and Twitter finally removed his account). But a corporation is free to follow its internal guidelines only when advantageous to do so, and to delete the president's account would have eliminated millions of "daily impressions"—the primary metric by which Twitter prices its ad space.

Despite the similarity to the *Time* cover, the frame of the president's tweet not only overshadows but eclipses what it holds. Each of the president's tweets is, in fact, all frame. To be looked at, this frame must constantly seek new content—relevance, accuracy, and consequences be damned. The contemporary ur-content, Trump's tweets are meaningless. They're not here for us to read, interpret, or understand. They exist to propagate the president himself, the reach of his personality. And of course they serve Twitter, Inc., the sole purpose of which is to generate profit for its shareholders. The president's Twitter account, before its deletion, was a totalitarian synergism, propagating a harmful, terrorizing personality for the sake of a corporation's profit, neither of which—the personality nor the profit—could afford stagnation.

∗∗∗

Like all content for content's sake, Donald Trump's is an aesthetic of noise. Meaningless by itself, noise needs context, or a frame, to become obfuscation, confusion, protest, agitation, terror, even torture (such as the CIA's weaponization of noise at Guantánamo Bay). The difference between the president and every other racist, misogynistic, tacky, ignorant, noisy, and mediocre bigot is his power. His influence over the law, the military, the courts, and a cult of unconditionally supportive, violent extremists is the context that transforms his adolescent thrashing into an optics of terror. The temptation, for our enjoyment, is to satirize Trump as a toddler who's found the family gun, unaware of its consequences, or to caricature him as a baby wiping his shit all over the American flag. This absolves him not only of responsibility but the guilt of taking pleasure in watching America grit its teeth as it waits for the bang. He knows that noise creates confusion and fear, and he knows that fear gets him what he wants. As a corporate entity, Donald Trump understands above all how to sell himself.

As loud as he is, the president can't make all this noise alone. Most of it comes from journalists, pundits, senators, representatives, and American citizens of every kind—rich and poor, educated and not, liberal and conservative, optimistically socialist and cynically fascist. Trump's tweets are analyzed (even for grammar and spelling), dissected, mocked, turned into memes, and quoted in both editorial pieces and reporting. Add this to *Saturday Night Live*, to casual conversation, to a glimpse of a TV at a bar, to Halloween costumes, and to every encounter with a social media platform of any kind, and it's clear that Trump content is everywhere. No other human being on earth has ever been this hideously omnipresent.

But despite all this content, few knew what the president was actually doing, and even fewer, what he planned to do. His administration's deployment of noise—as well as its amplification by supporters and critics alike—reduced our country to confusion and terror. In a democratic republic, a terrified and uninformed populace is robbed of the ability to govern itself.

Unfortunately, this dictatorship was the greatest single source of entertainment our nation has ever seen. We've long loved, it turns out, to be afraid.

***

On April 20, 1999, high school students Eric Harris and Dylan Klebold committed what was at that time an unimaginable act of terror. In a premeditated attack, the boys murdered twelve students and one teacher, injured twenty-four more, and killed themselves before police were able to enter the building. If you wish to be kind to yourself, you will not read about the details of their attack—what they said to students as they opened fire, what injuries those who survived have sustained, nor their demeanor as they walked from the school's cafeteria to the library to the science wing—nor will you read their journals, where they describe their ambition to rival the Oklahoma City bombing of 1995, both in scale and in terror. In scale, at least, the boys did not succeed.

While "Columbine" has entered the American vernacular—another atrocity-image hung on the walls of history—its unique, unprecedented horror is long forgotten. Equally forgotten is the media frenzy that followed, delving into the personalities, writings, friendships, and childhoods of Harris and Klebold. Ultimately, the boys became yet another cover image for *Time*. "The Monsters Next Door," reads the headline: "What Made Them Do It?"

Monsters are imaginary beings created out of fear. They are places, not people, and in them we relocate everything we and our society do not like. Another thing that's easy to forget, all these years later, is the monster this country chose to blame for Columbine, even though the killers did not like or listen to the band's music.

A year later, Marilyn Manson published an op-ed in *Rolling Stone* defending his choice to abstain from interviews about the shooting. Unfamiliar with KMFDM, a band the killers did praise, media networks focused on a highly visible and, at that time, incredibly controversial mainstream figure. By then, Manson himself had received several death threats, and had canceled the remainder of the band's tour to promote their 1998 album,

Mechanical Animals. "I think that the National Rifle Association is far too powerful to take on," he wrote, "so most people choose *Doom*, *The Basketball Diaries* or yours truly. This kind of controversy does not help me sell records or tickets, and I wouldn't want it to." Instead, Manson suggested, "media commentators [should] ask themselves [who is responsible], because their coverage of the event was some of the most gruesome entertainment any of us have seen." Despite the fury over the event, Manson lamented that "when these tragedies happen, most people don't really care any more than they would about the season finale of *Friends* or *The Real World*. I was dumbfounded as I watched the media snake right in, not missing a teardrop, interviewing the parents of dead children, televising the funerals." In a later interview, he reprised this indictment: "If you die and enough people are watching, then you become a martyr, you become a hero, you become well known. So when you have things like Columbine and you have these kids that are angry and they have something to say and no one's listening, the media sends a message that if you do something loud enough and it gets our attention, then you will be famous for it." In this, unfortunately, the boys did succeed.

In 2000, Manson's *Holy Wood* explored the celebrity achieved through martyrdom and death, including a quatrain about Columbine on "The Nobodies": "Some children died the other day / We fed machines and then we prayed / Puked up and down in morbid faith / You should've seen the ratings that day." Ironically, when the music video aired on MTV, the word "ratings" was censored.

In putting them on the cover of *Time*, said Manson, "The media gave them exactly what they wanted." There was never a question, not sincerely, of "What made them do it?" so much as an opportunity to invent some way that Harris and Klebold could be excluded from the human; and this makes them fascinating. Monsters are entrancing because there's always something we can't see, a darkness we can never access. Without monsters, we'd have to understand and empathize with how those we know and love—since no one we love could ever be a monster—might be capable of such terrible, unimaginable cruelties. Including, it must be said, the rock stars we used to see as heroes.

⁎⁎

The American monster inherits his otherness from Christianity. In the earliest centuries of the Church, as it distinguished itself from paganism by adapting Judaism's concept of idolatry, and later gained political favor by organizing and unifying its various sects, its theology began to shift from the societal to the individual. With Saint Augustine, in the fourth century, the prominence of the will—of the individual's determination over their own salvation— is almost modern: "And behold, Thou wert within, and I abroad, and there I searched for Thee; deformed I, plunging amid those fair forms which Thou hadst made. Thou wert with me, but I was not with Thee."

Especially remarkable is the sensuality with which Augustine imagines his reception of this Word: "Thou calledst and shoutedst, and burstest my deafness. Thou flashedst, shonest, and scatteredst my blindness. Thou breathedst odours, and I drew in breath and pant for Thee. I tasted, and hunger and thirst. Thou touchedst me, and I burned for Thy peace."

It is a choice, Augustine says, to look to and accept Christ as the Word made flesh; and this choice he recounts personally: "Only I had learnt out of what is delivered to us in writing of Him that He did eat, and drink, sleep, walk, rejoiced in spirit, was sorrowful, discoursed; that flesh did not cleave by itself unto Thy Word but with the human soul and mind." These pages, after all, are Augustine's *confessions*. Not only does he confess his rejoicing in the pleasures of the flesh, but so too his long, difficult, and solitary journey to renounce these pleasures.

From here, the development of Western philosophy throughout the centuries—Catholic, Protestant, and modern—adheres largely to the individual's place within and relationship to the greater world; the individual is the locus of philosophical engagement. One can trace, as Bertrand Russell does in his *History of Western Philosophy*, "the separation of clergy and laity" in the earliest centuries of Christianity to the modern-day remoteness of the intellectual or academic from "the average person," whoever that is; and it is this average person's task to decide for himself whether to follow the teachings of this clergy or these intellectuals, or to reject them. In addition, Russell argues, "modern philosophy, even when it is far from orthodox, is largely concerned with problems, especially in ethics and political theory, which are derived from Christian views of the moral law and from Catholic doctrines as to the relations of Church and State." At the same time, the Church concentrated more and more of its propaganda within the visual realm—an obvious choice with illiterate congregations. It is, ultimately, Christianity's iconographic aesthetic of martyrdom that creates the modern celebrity—the person so beloved and so remote that they elicit screams, hysteria, sobbing, and other sublime or ecstatic emotions in those who witness or experience them.

Where celebrity takes its monstrous turn is Romanticism, which took hold of the imagination just prior to the rise of the first democratic republics. As Russell describes it:

> Cultivated people in eighteenth-century France greatly admired what they called *la sensibilité*, which meant a proneness to emotion, and more particularly to the emotion of sympathy. To be thoroughly satisfactory, the emotion must be direct and violent and quite uninformed by thought. The man of sensibility would be moved to tears by the sight of a single destitute peasant family, but would be cold to well-thought-out schemes for ameliorating the lot of peasants as a class. The poor were supposed to possess more virtue than the rich; the sage was thought of as a man who retires from the corruption of the

courts to enjoy the peaceful pleasures of an unambitious rural existence.

With Romanticism, the imposition of the image upon the human is more obvious than ever, along with its political advantage for those in power. Obviously, if a man is supposed to be moved to tears by the sight of the poor, but too emotional to solve or address poverty, the poor become a useful gallery of morally charged images, especially for society's wealthiest and most powerful class. Aesthetics begins to subvert or obscure politics—all for the benefit of the few.

At the same time, Russell writes, the Romantics were obsessed with the strange: "ghosts, ancient decayed castles, the last melancholy descendants of once-great families, practitioners of mesmerism and the occult sciences, falling tyrants and levantine pirates." These are loners, outsiders. Mary Shelley's *Frankenstein* is the urtext of Romanticism, the first monster made by man. Whether by choice or by fate, "self-development was proclaimed as the fundamental principle of ethics." The hero is someone outside society— the prototype for the rock star, the rebel, the writer who shuns the industry, the actor who insults his colleagues, the men (they are always men) who behave badly because someone, somewhere, called them geniuses. Eventually, the hero's renunciation of social bonds becomes something to emulate; it is soon unromantic, and one day *uncool*, to care about societal structures, the needs of others, important causes. To be a hero is to be a monster. The 1990s, the last decade of the real rock stars—America's (and Britain's) monster-of-choice—was rife with this nihilism: no one, the story went, could ever make a difference, and the only way to protest the injustices of the world was to disengage—even, and often, to the point of suicide.

A culture of such concentrated celebrity—of martyrs and monsters—is a culture that values the self and its cultivation above all else, which doesn't seem so surprising in the United States, where our neighbors are suspicious and our coworkers are competitors. This can mean something like freedom, and in this country has carried freedom's destructive connotation. "The romantic movement," Russell writes, "aimed at liberating human personality from the fetters of social convention and social morality." In our celebrities, we place everything we either can't bring ourselves to be (the martyrs) or can't bear to acknowledge in ourselves (the monsters).

***

You should've seen the ratings that day: They are to television what click counters and impressions are to online content. If you are a writer, these clicks quantify your worth in the eyes of those who decide to pay you, be it in cash or exclamation marks. Both are measures of how many eyes have seen the frame of advertisements that surrounds your editorial, artistic, or journalistic content. When ratings and clicks begin to influence the editorial direction of that which is placed in this frame, it becomes sensationalism.

Manson himself, whose entire career was built out of "shock," controversy, and art direction, is no stranger to this concept. With the 1996 release of *Antichrist Superstar*, Manson became a household name and media darling. All these years later, it's hard to intimate to someone who wasn't there just how ubiquitous Marilyn Manson really was, and how, at that time, the band brought mainstream music into a new theatrics of gruesome images, scandalous costumes, and music videos thenceforth unimagined by most American viewers and listeners. And this is exactly what made him a scapegoat (and not, of course, his horrific, ultimately abusive treatment of women) after the Columbine massacre: "America loves to find an icon to hang its guilt on," he wrote in *Rolling Stone*. "Admittedly, I have assumed the role of Antichrist ... In my work I examine the America we live in, and I've always tried to show people that the devil we blame our atrocities on is really just each one of us." For Manson, sensationalism was an artful indulgence. Even the band's name, a compound of Marilyn Monroe and Charles Manson, reflects this critique of "the sad fact that America puts killers on the cover of *Time Magazine*, giving them as much notoriety as our favorite movie stars." His legacy, or what's left of it, only makes sense in a country that embraces the theater of atrocity, which inevitably comes to rely on atrocity itself: the content required by the form of being horrifically entertained.

In the sensationalist newsroom, truth is subservient to profit. This is not a new or controversial argument; any reader or viewer with half a conscience knows that news is calibrated toward clicks, views, retweets, shares, and any other buzz it can generate. Even the arrangement of articles in a newspaper or on a web page reveals that publication's allegiance to revenue. This is a key part of Noam Chomsky and Edward Herman's "propaganda model," wherein large media organizations find it advantageous to reduce and restrict news coverage to a relatively small, easy-to-follow mainstream narrative. This is borne of a variety of factors, including "ownership and control, dependence on other major funding sources (notably, advertisers), and mutual interests and relationships between the media and those who make the news." These work in concert to deprive the majority of Americans (as well as citizens of other capitalist nations) of the facts necessary to make informed political judgments. As Chomsky observed in a 1976 interview with Mitsou Ronat, disseminating an official version of events is more effective

> when its doctrines are insinuated rather than asserted, when it sets the bounds for possible thought rather than simply imposing a clear and easily identifiable doctrine that one must parrot . . . Hence the elaborate pretense that the press is a critical

dissenting force ... when in fact it is almost entirely subservient to the basic principles of the ideological system: in this case, the principle right of the United States to serve as global judge and executioner.

Through the lens of the propaganda model, one sees how the media repeatedly frames its coverage—not consciously, but through constraints put in place by factors mentioned above—to flatter the financial interests of those in power. Meanwhile, people who read the news—especially news that seems critical of the government—feel as if they can independently form intelligent, rational opinions about events taking place in their country and communities. This is most clear in matters of war, which is largely unfavorable in the eyes of most Americans, yet a longtime favorite of mainstream media. Even Donald Trump only has to bomb a faraway, nonwhite nation to become "presidential" in the eyes of *New York Times* reporters. Though small in number, many powerful Americans earn their billions from ongoing conflict, and rely on media to portray that conflict as just, no matter how many lives are lost.

It's not radical, either, to say that this prioritization of profit by major media organizations—including *The New York Times*, CNN, MSNBC, and others labeled as liberal—is what skewed the discourse leading up to the 2016 election, as well as how each candidate was perceived. The majority of coverage Clinton received cast her as untrustworthy and unlikeable, a professional candidate who would do little to change American politics. Trump, on the other hand, was portrayed as a dangerous and inexperienced wild card; nearly every article was written in sensational disbelief. Most front-page, top-circulated stories centered on Trump and his outlandish, "anti-establishment" behavior. Indeed, for a while it was hard to gauge Clinton's policies at all, despite knowing from the beginning each and every lie Trump fed his fan base. Morally and politically, the choice was clear as soon as each was nominated, but media organizations inflated one candidate's untrustworthiness to match it against her fascinating opponent; otherwise, there would have been no conflict to beckon buying eyes to the ads.

Once elected, Trump and his fascist administration became the dominant news story every single day. While polling lower than any president in history, his performance seems irrelevant—or perhaps adversely correlative—to journalists' collective refusal to look away. If presidencies had ratings rather than performance polls, his would be the most-watched, most-consumed, and highest-rated administration in world history. Which, despite a dearth of successful policy implementation, might explain this reality TV star's insistence that his presidency was the most successful of any president before him. Before *The Apprentice*, Trump was a creature of the tabloids who gossiped about his marriages, his divorces, where he was seen in Manhattan, and what he'd done that week. Most of these stories were called into magazines directly, supposedly by Trump's publicist—either a "John Miller" or a "John Barron"— but in reality by Trump himself, trying to disguise his voice. His entire life is an affair with publicity, sensationalism, and attention: Why should anyone expect him to feel as though he's failed? The American public, though thoroughly terrified, has never been as enthralled, as engaged, or as entertained with its president. The spectacle of Donald Trump gives each of us a clear, definable stake, and we—no matter our political alignment—are made to feel we can defend it simply by watching.

***

In David Shields's *Reality Hunger*, readers are invited to believe that, over the centuries, what Western critics call fact and what they call fiction have gradually borrowed from one another, and that, in the twenty-first century, there is little need to separate them: "The techniques of fiction infected history; the materials of history were fed to the novelist's greed." In part, Shields defends his self-described manifesto—which extends little beyond his personal boredom with the novel as an art form—with the rise of "reality" in entertainment, especially television, which does away with the pretense of scripts, scenery, character, and plot, though in fact relies upon all of these elements in a subversive way. Reality TV, as we've come to know it, is a far cry from the first seasons of *The Real World*, in which participants spent most of their time sleeping or eating in front of a closed-circuit network of grainy surveillance cameras.

Almost three decades later, reality TV is more formulaic than the prime-time sitcom ever was, and far more predictable than whatever iteration of *Law & Order* is currently on the air. Characters (selected by producers to form a matrix of opposing personalities) fight, scheme, gossip, cry, throw drinks, form allegiances, and, in general, get quite comfortable under their network of surveillance, performing yet never acting. That one never need know the exact circumstances behind a garden-variety reality show, yet still be drawn into it, speaks to the producers' innate

While the premise of reality TV is new, it's the soap opera—narratives in serial even in the heyday of episodic television—from which "reality" borrows its tropes: natural enemies; long-standing grudges; the elimination of beloved characters; characters who reappear, seasons later, with fanfare and surprise; and constant cliff-hangers. And it's these tropes that have dispensed with traditional episodic TV. America's most talked-about shows for the last twenty years have been narratives in serial, including *Lost*, *Battlestar Galactica*, *Game of Thrones*, *Orange Is the New Black*, and many more.

talent to find a character whom every viewer can relate to, whether through adoration, hatred, jealousy, or schadenfreude. It succeeds as a genre entirely on the basis of personality. With *Survivor* in the late nineties, the introduction of elimination only galvanized this character-driven narrative: with each episode, your favorite personality was at risk of being voted off the show. In the early 2000s, this suspenseful model propagated itself with competition-based shows like *American Idol*, *The Bachelor*, *America's Next Top Model*, *Top Chef*, and of course *The Apprentice*. All are contests to be the most noticeable, the most celebrity-like, of contestants.

Here are a handful of sign-offs the former president of the United States used on his former Twitter account: "Big changes are happening!" "We will deliver!" "Did Hillary know?" "The real story." "Find the leakers." "Much higher ratings at Fox." "We will see what happens!" He may as well tweet, *Stay tuned!* With unconstitutional executive orders, surprise bombings, revolving door White House staff, and relentless antagonism of everyone who doesn't adore him, it should surprise no one that Trump ran his administration as a reality show. His stupidity and the banality of his language reduces him to a catalogue of catchphrases—"We'll see," "Fake news," "Witch hunt"—which are magnetic for his fans and repellent for those who rightfully despise him. But few can look away. This interest—this fascination—in Trump seems compulsory, a need to reassure oneself that the unbelievable is really happening, that such a sensational satire of cruelty and incompetence is becoming reality. Meanwhile, by the time he was inaugurated, the news cycle had accelerated to a continuous narrative, related in real time. No breaks, no seasons, no episodes: just one unending cliffhanger, with all of us wondering whether or not we'd die in a nuclear war before he left office.

And of course, like other criminals, he fit neatly on the cover of *Time*.

With Trump, reality TV and reality itself have melded. Unsurprisingly, this serial abuser has found a way to remove consent from viewership. He is the character who's forced his way into each of our lives, and it's impossible to tune him out. In this way, he has achieved through the manipulation of media what Manson could not. While Manson's reflection of hypocrisy draws a line between artifice and reality (or at least it did until very serious allegations of abuse, even torture, came out against him), Trump has blurred that line; it's no longer possible to tell whether or not Trump believes a single thing he says, or if a life of inhabiting an image has erased whatever personhood was once underneath. If Marilyn Manson *played* America's antichrist, Trump seems to be it—the American monster par excellence.

This explains the temptation to dissect his psychology, or to propose that he's playing some sort of political chess. From the perspective of American citizens, there is nothing beyond this performance. Despite all the articles, essays, and books that try to delve into his personality, there is nothing that indicates a human being behind this spectacle. In all grippingly operatic television, the character sincerely believes in the drama in which he is living. He believes in the righteousness of his actions. As Mark Doten put it in his novel *Trump Sky Alpha*: "If I have to die, shouldn't everyone?" To pretend otherwise—to *not* take him at his word—is not just disingenuous and irresponsible; in trying to read a subtext that isn't there—in looking beyond an image that's lost its real-world referent—journalists and pundits risk, more than ever, getting someone, maybe everyone, killed.

***

Donald Trump is not an anomaly. He is merely a breakthrough in a business model reliant upon terror. Fear has long served profit and power at the expense of society. Deployed by politicians and amplified by strategic media programming, fear increasingly came to influence the American citizen's consumption of news throughout the twentieth century, but it wasn't until the U.S. War on Terror that fear attained unprecedented currency.

In the United States, terror is profitable. On the morning that Trump became president-elect, we spent money: flags, T-shirts, newspapers, magazines, political organizations, support to Planned Parenthood, passport applications, and Xanax. Prescriptions and subscriptions went up; the DOW and NASDAQ climbed with them. But this had all happened before. One need look no further than 9/11 to see terror's value in selling not just flags and stickers but ideology.

Two decades later, reading or thinking about those early days after 9/11 is as painful as seeing the towers appear in films, on album covers, or in photographs. The lingering terror—at least for me—is no longer the image of lives lost, though that's certainly a disturbing part of our history. Instead, the lingering terror is the conditional past, what we could have done in response to 9/11. Juxtaposed with liberties lost under the Patriot Act, the DHS, the TSA, Guantánamo and its siblings, the NSA, the practice of torture, on and on—not to mention the cost, human and otherwise, of ongoing war—the image of our country that could have been, had we chosen to grieve responsibly, is almost too great to bear. Already, there are young people who have no memory of what it was like to live in, ostensibly, a non-surveillance state where a person could travel without a government employee openly violating their constitutional rights.

Eerily, 11/9 is now another demarcation in time, redolent with its own irretrievable conditions and could-have-beens. But given the enthusiasm of many Trump supporters, who seem to believe that securing an already-militarized border is worth surrendering what remains of our rights, this country has, so far, learned nothing from 9/11 but the euphoria of submission. This neutering of the will has always been fascism's appeal, as Hannah Arendt writes in *The Origins of Totalitarianism*: "Both the early apathy and the later demand for monopolistic dictatorial direction of the nation's foreign affairs had their roots in a way and philosophy of life so insistently and exclusively centered on the individual's success or failure in ruthless competition that a citizen's duties and responsibilities could only be felt to be a needless drain on his limited time and energy." With Trump, it's increasingly obvious that authoritarian control is the last hope of an exhausted, impoverished, unhealthy electorate that no longer wishes to exercise its citizenship. As a nation, we no longer want to lead, to think, to vote, or even to believe that things can change; we only want to be told what to do, and for those orders to be as entertaining as possible.

**

In his analysis of image technology and military engagement, *War and Cinema*, Paul Virilio posits that war itself is waged by sight: "From the original watch-tower through the anchored balloon to the reconnaissance aircraft and remote-sensing satellites, one and the same function has been indefinitely repeated, the eye's function being the function of a weapon."

With the exception of soldiers who've been there and civilians who've lived under fire, the public understanding of war is an understanding of images. Our image vocabulary of war is a lexicon of photographs, video clips, cinematic narratives, and journalistic snapshots of *what it was like*. In our apocalyptic daydreams, we can even picture—thanks to fifty years of Hollywood blockbusters—what it might be like to lose our flesh in a nuclear instant, to witness our cities burned off the earth. But that, Virilio notes, wasn't always the case:

> There is no war, then, without representation, no sophisticated weaponry without psychological mystification . . . In this respect the first atomic bombs, dropped on Hiroshima and Na-

gasaki on the 6th and 9th of August 1945, presented the ideal conditions: great mechanical effectiveness, complete technical surprise, but, above all, the moral shock that suddenly banished to the prop-room the earlier strategic carpet-bombing of large Asian and European cities, with all its logistical sluggishness. By demonstrating that they would not recoil from a civilian holocaust, the Americans triggered in the minds of the enemy that information explosion which Einstein, towards the end of his life, thought to be as formidable as the atomic blast itself.

To this day, the United States is the only nation to deploy nuclear weaponry against another. Those two hundred thousand civilians remain the only civilians deliberately murdered in an atomic blast. The scale of this image has lodged itself deeply in the contemporary imagination. Like the outlines of bodies burned onto Hiroshima's sidewalks and buildings (the same principle as photography), this is a shadow this light has cast. Often I wonder what the latter half of the twentieth century would have been like without the bomb. Its image informs our art and literature, our cinema and advertising and publicity. For those who live in that shadow, it's not hard to conclude that the United States, in August of 1945, committed the greatest, most heinous act of terrorism in human history. Even today, we have yet to reckon with this, or officially acknowledge it.

Not only did Trump reprise the world's nuclear anxiety after a post-Soviet respite—officially withdrawing, in February 2019, from the 1987 Intermediate-Range Nuclear Forces Treaty—but it now coexists with the collective imagination of ecological ruin. The glaciers of Greenland are hemorrhaging almost two million gallons of fresh water into the sea every second. In 2015, the northern white rhino was declared technically extinct. Across the globe, coral reefs are bleaching and dying. In the early days of Japan's Fukushima disaster, approximately 520 tons of radioactive water spilled into the sea and contaminated the entire Pacific Ocean. What is being done? Who is taking action? In 2016, honeybees were added to the endangered species list; as I write this, it's still legal for the agricultural industry to use pesticides that lead to colony collapse disorder.

Bees, in fact, are dying globally at an alarming rate—so much so that it's become a meme, as Lauren Duca writes for *The New Inquiry*. Most of these memes show an individual removed, emotionally, from his or her circumstances—at the club or a dinner with friends, at house parties, at sporting events. The turning inward one could read as a form of distraction: the subject was having a good time until they remembered that bees were dying. But so too could one read the subject's face as a sudden suspension from distraction—an instantaneous confrontation with reality. In this sense, the meme becomes a meta-meme, a reference to the ways we distract ourselves to cope with the cascade of news pushed to our phones every day: inexplicable worldwide violence; absurd pronouncements by cartoonish politicians; legislation that unabashedly favors the wealthy; a new extinction; another landmark or beach or island lost; and someday, not far off, entire cities abandoned. As Duca observes of the bees: "There is nothing we can do about it. Or maybe there is something we can do about it? But we won't. The hopelessness attached to either possibility is great for comedy." The loudness of our laughter is a wish to drown out all that other awful noise; we entertain ourselves with co-opted terror because there is only so much real terror a person can process before they adapt, before it becomes something to use rather than something to feel. Each day, something immeasurably terrible happens; each day, I think of Christa Wolf's note in her diary, in 1981:

> On the sixth of August, the anniversary of the day the bomb was dropped on Hiroshima, the American President made the

decision to build the neutron bomb; the Secretary of Defense revealed that the first warheads have been mounted and could be in Western Europe in a few hours in case they were needed there. This could be our death sentence, I thought; but what did I really feel? Helplessness. I put breakfast on the table in the yard. Talked with the others. Laughed.

As with the imposition of the nuclear imagination in the latter half of the twentieth century, everything Trump is doing—even out of office—seems calibrated toward reminding the entire world, at every opportunity, of its tenuous future. If a future you could call it. What we're seeing as Trump divides this nation, as he incites more violence, is exactly what we expected to see from the moment he announced his candidacy.

And we are meant to see it. Trump's supporters assaulting women and minorities in the streets on the morning of 11/9: we're meant to see it. We're meant to notice that every person Trump assigns to oversee a branch of the federal government is the ideal person to subvert and dissolve that department. We're meant to understand the consequences of a renewed nuclear arms race. We're meant to panic at his every denial of reality, and the mainstream media's shoulder-shrugging at every new lie or unsupported claim. We're meant, as an easily preventable pandemic ravages the nation, to watch helplessly alongside a hamstrung CDC as hundreds of thousands of Americans die. During the election, it seemed impossible that Trump could win—not only for his ignorance of politics, economics, and foreign policy, but for his sheer, unfiltered hatred of women, Black and Indigenous Americans, people of color, persons with disabilities, immigrants, journalists, and anyone who's ever read a book. This story was supposed to be different. Hillary Clinton, under whose governance we would be "stronger together," was supposed to triumph over hatred, stupidity, violence. Yes, I fell for this, and if you're reading this you probably did too. From the point of view of Trump and his supporters, her loss was meant to feel hopeless. You and I were supposed to feel like America was no longer for us.

All of this is intentional because Donald Trump is a terrorist. His election to the U.S. presidency is a domestic terrorist attack planned and coordinated by white supremacists. However, he could not have done this without the psychological warfare corporations have waged for decades, hammering into the American consciousness that money is what matters, that the rich will always win, despite all the propaganda to the contrary—our films and TV shows and stories where the rich get their comeuppance. Trump is proof, despite what is right and good in the world, that money and cruelty and stupidity can win. What is this if not terror?

Of course, my personal terror is borne of my privilege as a white man living in a systemically racist society. And it's here, in this contradiction—in this "sudden" dawn of terror that was no shock to those who've lived their entire lives in "Trump's America"—that our nation faces its greatest opportunity, that we can learn what we failed to learn after 9/11.

In Trump's embodiment of everything that is wrong with America—and everything that has been wrong since its founding— we are forced to see the work that needs to be done. We are forced to reckon with our nation's legacy of preying upon all other nations; with its systemic and racist inequality, its poverty, its abominable education system, its vanity, and its poor health; and most of all, with its fatal equating of individual wealth, glamour, and celebrity to moral superiority, to greatness. There can be no more pretending that the United States is exceptional or innocent. We're out of wool to pull over our eyes.

Unless of course you're one of Trump's loyalists. For these people, pretending is all there is. Fascism's deepest appeal is a schism from reality. It not only bristles against the contradictions of a complex society but actively erases them, installing fictions in their place. In *Totalitarianism*, Arendt describes the masses' "longing for fiction," which stems from "those capacities of the human mind whose structural consistency is superior to mere occurrence." As a society begins to neglect more and more of its individuals, fascism's simplicity—its one-dimensional narrative—gains traction: "The masses' escape from reality is a verdict against the world in which they are forced to live and in which they cannot exist, since coincidence has become its supreme master and human beings need the constant transformation of chaotic and accidental conditions into a man-made pattern of relative consistency." As mentioned above—and in various vocabularies—shock and atrocity are followed by reductive simplicity, by storybook narratives. When the terrorist attack is domestic—when those terrorized live alongside those who seek to inspire terror—our acceptance of these narratives isn't so immediate, nor so conformist.

This is a complexity that must be embraced, not reduced. To dispose of Trump and call our work done would be to make a monster of him, to place everything awful about America on his hunched shoulders and cast him out; and we would be reborn, we would be innocent again, and our story would start over with new characters, new atrocities, new monsters. But getting rid of Trump still leaves us with the country that not only elected him but created him. Instead, what needs to be resisted is the production and consumption of terror in exchange for profit, not to mention the usage of martyrs and monsters as repositories for the extreme states of humanity, for our ecstasy and our terror. Giving into a role assigned to you from without—be it "resistance fighter," "real American," or simply an indistinct part of a terrified populace—only entrenches these narratives. We trap ourselves neatly in a story that makes someone else rich, often destroying the lives of others—if not ourselves—in the process.

The stakes of the United States of America as it exists are easy to identify. Human beings are dying, at home and abroad, so someone can scare us for money. Without intervention, this will continue until everyone, everywhere, is dead. This is not hyperbole.

If modern warfare, in Virilio's words, provides us with a situation where "the image (photographic or cinematic) is the most concentrated, but also the most stable, form of information," images themselves, deployed for sensation, become weaponized. Images of helpless women become images of terror. Images of Black victims without convicted murderers are terror. Images of the wealthy and their armored, imperious glamour while the poor die of treatable diseases are terror. The president laughing about sexual assault is terror. Images of his promise to dissolve every federal protection we have: terror. Images of unchallenged ecological disaster, of floods, fires, drought—all terror. Images of my generation as lazy, entitled, doomed, all while we work harder than our parents only to fall further behind every day—I don't doubt for a second that these are terror. Juxtaposed with images of the past—housing that was once affordable, tuition you could pay with a part-time job, and a planet that wasn't yet, as we are every day now told, irrevocably damaged—this is terror at its most elemental: *It's inconvenient that you exist*, these images say, *and it would be preferable if you never had.*

It's no wonder Americans are so afraid, and that so many seek to surrender their will to dictatorial control. Only a child is afraid of everything. Only a child demands protection from every absurd, imagined fear. Only a child's stories lack complexity. By choosing to regress into innocence, to hide from its own crimes, that is exactly what this country makes of itself: a child whose tantrums kill by the thousands, by the millions; whose wailing in the dark is drowning countries on the other side of the earth, and whose reck-less pushing of buttons could announce the end of humanity itself.

These stories must end. This country must switch off its cartoon politics and embrace complexity, heterogeneity, even contradictions. We must abandon the childish belief that the individual as an isolated being is somehow virtuous. We must take care of our own and others in every way. We must resist our fictions and accept ourselves as we are: not only broken and vulnerable, but still powerful, still capable—and, above all, ready to grieve what we've lost as we create something new.

> How does someone propose to speak the
> truth about Fascism, to which he is op-
> posed, if he does not propose to speak out
> against capitalism, which produces it?
>
> —BERTOLT BRECHT, 1935

In the United States, the cultural connotations of fascism and totalitarianism are derived from this country's historic (and most dramatic, most spectacular) political adversaries: Nazi Germany and Soviet Russia. Sometimes, one may picture this or that Latin American junta from the seventies or eighties, but rarely with the awareness of who installed and empowered those dictators. In all cases, fascism and totalitarianism are supposed to sound exotically horrifying. Often, they serve as images in and of themselves.

These other regimes are easy for Americans to grasp—not to mention fear. Our entertainment is full of them; along with the atom bomb, the totalitarian threat sparks more film plots and thriller novels throughout the twentieth century than any other historic scenario, if not all others combined. Unsurprisingly, they've found a new audience in the twenty-first century, either via television adaptations or simply new novels and films. As with most forms of entertainment, particularly those branded or categorized as art forms, there is a shadow-understanding that they will "instruct" or "prepare," or at the very least familiarize, viewers and readers and listeners with what a totalitarian politics in power looks like. Nearly all of them have left us just as ignorant as before. This is, again, a matter of images and their situated contexts, their space and their time—as well as who creates and distributes those images for our consumption.

One word, then, to describe Guillermo Saccomanno's novel *77*—translated into English by Andrea G. Labinger in 2019—is "timely." We could learn something, as American readers, from Saccomanno's claustrophobic rendering of Jorge Rafael Videla's Argentina. In that country's past, where CIA-funded terror suppressed leftist politics with nine years of torture, murder, kidnappings, rape, surveillance, and intimidation, we could recognize a warning of what nationalism can become in our own country, where *socialism* has, for a hundred years, been a cipher for all things treason.

I only say "could" because we've had hundreds, if not thousands, of other opportunities—some artistically better, most of them worse—to learn these same lessons, to edify as we entertain ourselves. The other word I could use, with respect to *77*'s effect on an American reading public, is "irrelevant." Opportunities like these require a will to learn, and given the fact that few in this nation seemed to care about Videla's junta when it existed—nor the tens of thousands killed and hundreds of thousands extrajudicially imprisoned—is a lesson in comfort and complicity. The only thing that's timely about a novel like *77* is how uncomfortable Americans have become on their own soil, how suddenly sensitive to the idea of fascism's encroachment upon reality, even if it is, as I've said, more entertaining in our day-to-day lives than it ever was in the movies.

Nonetheless, I do think the novel is worth a close look. It takes its title from that year, following Videla's military coup in 1976. Argentina is entrenched in terror. Police kidnap people in broad daylight; rarely are they seen again. No one interferes: "We passengers avoided making eye contact. No one had seen anything. Maybe I hadn't, either." Into this, Saccomanno plunges Gómez, a middle-aged high school professor of English literature who cruises the alleyways of Buenos Aires for public sex with younger men. "As many people as necessary must die in Argentina so that the country will again be secure," Videla said in 1975—the real Videla. As with any totalitarian system, this "as necessary" never stops moving. "The military issued an announcement," Gómez remembers, telling his story to an unspeci-
fied narrator thirty years after it happened: "First we will elimi-nate the subversives, then their

In this one hears an echo of Arendt's warning that "Totalitarianism strives not toward despotic rule over men, but toward a system in which men are superfluous."

accomplices, then their sympathizers, and finally all those who are indifferent or lukewarm."

"Terror makes a person more cunning," Gómez says. "Not more intelligent, more cunning. Like a fox that evades the hunting party. But that survival skill, when it's honed, becomes madness." Like any humanist, he believes in literature—in poetry and in art. Gómez finds moments to laugh and to flirt. He enjoys reading and hot tea and getting fucked in the ass by strangers. He is living in a system that, ideologically, says he cannot exist; and like most Argentines he lives in it quietly: "If a military raid shook the night with explosions, gunshots, shrieks, and babies' screams, the neighborhood soothed its conscience by thinking there must have been a reason." He is the ideal subject of totalitarian rule: that is, neutral.

His old friends and new friends demand his sympathetic ear: they've turned to poetry, they tell him; they've turned to the occult; they cut photographs of Videla from the newspapers and pierce his eyes and slip them into the locked bedrooms of their disappeared children. No one is a safe confidant because everyone is a liability. Anyone can be tortured, even Gómez himself, despite harboring, in his apartment, two people he comes to love very much: "To escape," he admits, "I would name anyone."

A necessity of tyranny is this isolation, this atomization of individuals into solitaries unable to love or trust one another. Tyranny cannot exist, as Arendt writes, "without destroying the public realm of life, that is, without destroying, by isolating men, their political capacities." A step beyond tyranny, totalitarian rule, Arendt says, "destroys private life as well [as public]. It bases itself on loneliness, on the experience of not belonging to the world at all." In loneliness, "man loses trust in himself as the partner of his thoughts and that elementary confidence in the world which is necessary to make experiences at all."

Another necessity of tyranny is submission. If you don't fall on your knees, psychologically, and feverishly welcome Videla's regime, you might fall on your literal knees and choke, as Gómez often does, on a corrupt cop's dick while he pulls your hair. You might surrender your will to the spirits who will help locate your missing child. You might travel deep into the provinces to visit a psychic. You might hand over your life to an armed resistance with dogmas of its own. You might abandon thought and speak in metaphors that flatten other human beings, or you might, like Gómez, abdicate to literature itself, which "in its pretension, confused history with the activity of bodies and the conclusions that could be drawn from their behavior." Societies most vulnerable to fascist or totalitarian rule are already in some way damaged, peopled by the exhausted, the worn out, the lonely and afraid—by those who wish to hand their life to someone or something else, whoever or whatever promises to say, *I'll fix this*. You might, in twenty-first century America, find refuge in memes or in hats with slogans.

You might turn to the angriest pundit and call them the voice of reason.

Above all, tyranny requires terror: "Terror took over," Gómez tells his interlocutor, "first in small matters, until it invaded even basic language functions, the language of thought, the language of speech, written language, body language, each and every gesture." Terror isolates. It is the totalitarian separator, its highest form of governance to which one either submits or resists—either way under threat of total erasure. As American readers coming to a novel like *77*—or Kertész's *Fatelessness* or Sebald's *Austerlitz* or Serge's *Unforgiving Years* or Némirovsky's *Suite Française* or Neruda's poetry or García Márquez's banana plantation massacre—shouldn't we already know that? Have we learned nothing of terror after centuries on this continent, stenciling our fears onto others, isolating ourselves, submitting to harmful and stupid ideologies? Have we not created a cheerful, expensive—even *fun*—loneliness like no other in history, and has it not damaged us? It should be no surprise at all that we've opted, at last, to surrender to a dictator.

But in truth we surrendered long ago, and to a totalitarian claim on the imagination that is far subtler, and far harder to see, than any of the spectacular regimes that populate our entertainment. A necessary project is to make this system visible. As novelist Daša Drndić once said, "There are no small fascisms."

***

Another magazine cover: In February of 2019, *Esquire* published "The Life of an American Boy at 17." Ryan Morgan, the subject of this profile, is not the kind of American boy a police officer could get away with murdering, nor the kind who kills himself because his parents send him to a camp that tortures him into loving differently. In fact, the magazine seemed to have chosen Ryan as a provocation or dog whistle, as if to reinforce the presumed, blank whiteness of "American boy" in a nation where many boys are not white, and in fact nothing like Ryan.

Words, though, are not blank; "American" and "boy" are not white. But it is their history, their usage, and their context in this country that make them feel otherwise. When this history and context are overlooked or taken for granted, especially in mainstream publications, that bias can leap off the page and affect the way people live, or die. The way writing—especially journalistic writing—is taught and evaluated helps reinforce this bias. According to the mainstream criteria of journalism, Jennifer Percy's article is well written; she is almost entirely invisible. Only once does she intrude, as the author, to challenge what Ryan says—his minimizing remark about baseball player Josh Hader's homophobia. It's the only part of the piece that stakes an ethical claim. Otherwise, Percy leaves uninterrogated Ryan's support for capital punishment, his stance against abortion and safe sex, his misogynistic views on the social roles of boys and girls, and several other beliefs that, as he enters his local polling place for the first time, will affect real people's lives.

Instead, we are meant to form our own opinions about who Ryan is and "what it means" for a seventeen-year-old straight white boy in a conservative municipality of Wisconsin to have these views. Thus, the piece is written as if Ryan is an unfamiliar or exotic subject for profiling when in fact he is the institutionally approved median, or "neutral," of young masculinity in the United States. Ryan is at the center of two centuries of culture, entertainment, law, education, art, and politics. This country was built, mostly by enslaved people, for boys like him.

I, for example, have always known who he is, because Ryan is the model I was supposed to imitate—at least until my sexuality got in the way. It's not only insulting that a mainstream publication assumes I can't see him—that any queer, any person of color, or any girl or woman, can't see him. It's cruel. And it seems a deliberate cruelty, because all *Esquire* did was re-emphasize this neutrality, this apparent normative ideal, against which the rest of us read as un-American.

Clinging to a false neutrality like this only strengthens the ideologies of whiteness and male chauvinism. Percy may not have written this propaganda on purpose, but neither is Ryan, *on purpose*, a bigot whose unchallenged ignorance can and will harm other people. This is what people mean when they lament the inevitability of "the system": Percy is doing what the system asks of her—recording what happened and who said what—and doing it well. Ryan is behaving like the boy the system wants him to be. Jay Fielden, *Esquire*'s editor at the time, proved equally faithful to this system, in which words are supposed to be transparent, self-propagating tools of something called civilization. They are, we are taught by this system, objective.

Like any ethically unmoored aesthetics, these are behaviors and beliefs modeled after imitation, even play. We imitate forms of beauty, for example, because those are the forms our culture calls beautiful, and then we call those imitations beautiful. This is how genres come about—images cleaved from one another and labeled, which seems to be not only the great project of Western art but of Western civilization. These words—genre, order, species, class, medium, gender, archetype, trope—and many like them are the legacy of European thought, which has named, ranked, divided, and classified nearly all of human experience, and placed it in jars of formaldehyde. "American boy," for American readers, connotes someone like Ryan thanks to centuries of this kind of thinking.

In these systems of classification, what starts as science spills into politics, ethics, art, and even, via Freud, our imaginations. Freud's temptation, as one of history's great mythographers, was to diagnose all personalities, to excise each from an illusory normality to which no one is bland or blank enough to belong, and then pathologize civilization itself: "The super-ego of an epoch of civilization has an origin similar to that of an individual . . . May we not be justified in reaching the diagnosis that, under the influence of cultural urges, some civilizations, or some epochs of civilization—possibly the whole of mankind—have become 'neurotic'?" Immensely creative—a genius of pattern recognition—Freud applied a scientific vocabulary to the literary or mythological imagination, erasing and rewriting real personalities belonging to real individuals. Like Marx or Hegel, he created a total system; anything can be assimilated into its definitions.

Adhering to Freud's mythography are the archetypists, whose work, while seductive, is predicated entirely on this erasure of individual life. In 1990, Camille Paglia published *Sexual Personae*, the first of two volumes of psychoanalytically saturated art history. Her insistence on gender performance, identifying men with Apollo and women with Dionysus, celebrates subjugation and destruction: "Male bonding and patriarchy were the recourse to which man was forced by his terrible sense of woman's power . . . Woman's body is a labyrinth in which man is lost." Of

After reading Paglia (which is horrifying but rarely boring), it's no longer possible to be shocked by the rhetoric of reactionary movements. Autocratic populism, white supremacy, misogyny, and other bigotries are one-dimensional theories that, on paper, create the illusion that the complexities of human life would disappear if everyone would stick to their role, regardless of how or by whom such roles—sex, race, creed, blood—are assigned and policed.

course, she adds, not all men ruin themselves over their desire for women's confusing and terrifying bodies: "By turning away from the Medusan mother, whether in honor or detestation of her, the male homosexual is one of the great forgers of absolutist Western identity. But of course nature has won, as she always does, by making disease the price of promiscuous sex." (Since the HIV epidemic began, more than forty million human beings have died of AIDS-related illnesses.)

Like Freud, Paglia has no interest in the individual except as canvas. This obsession with reduction, with the taxonomy of sex and art, reaches its "economic glorification in capitalism," or "the mysticism and glamour of *things*, which take on a personality of their own." Capitalism, she writes, "is one of the greatest male accomplishments in the history of culture."

Sexual Personae vol. 2 has yet to be published.

The path away from Freud is more interesting, and more difficult. If, in Paglia's consciousness, the "thingness" of human existence is glorified, in Simone de Beauvoir's it is abhorred. "Along with the ethical urge of each individual to affirm his subjective existence," she writes in *The Second Sex*, "there is also the temptation to forego liberty and become a thing." To accept one's objectification by a dominant culture is to accept one's otherness. Culture itself is built on this reciprocity: "Males could not enjoy [their] privilege unless they believed it to be founded on the absolute and the eternal . . . Legislators, priests, philosophers, writers, and scientists have striven to show that the subordinate position of woman is willed in heaven and advantageous on earth." As the political, economic, and biological sciences advanced, they too were co-opted and deployed to reflect these supremacist ideologies, and at great profit to those in power: "One of the benefits that oppression confers upon the oppressors is that the most humble among them is made to *feel* superior . . . The most mediocre of males feels himself a demigod as compared with women."

For de Beauvoir, there's no such thing as "eternal" values: "Every objective description, so called, implies an ethical background." It's here where Freud's ethical compass, after a lifetime of imposing identities, neuroses, and mythologies—particularly upon women—becomes nothing but a gnarl of projections meant to disable, disbar, delineate, and depress. Even today, when biology or chemistry are deployed as objective truth, it's with a subjective and limited ethics: implying that gender is biological destiny, for example, or that same-sex relationships are unnatural because they cannot provide children. This is also (if less harmfully) fallacious from the opposing viewpoint—pointing to gay penguins, for example, as a scientific defense of homosexuality, or toward the neurological mapping of emotions as a way to prove literature has value in a consumerist society. Assigning chief epistemological importance to any one category of knowledge only means that whoever controls the category controls the culture—and who gets to live and thrive within it. Applied to any philosophical or technological system, the label "objective" is just a claim to ownership: *This structure is meant for me, not for you.*

***

The photographer's compulsion echoes the pathologist's—using the limits of the frame to separate this landscape from that, the self from its environment, and to call it the truth. But just as it is with ideologies, there is no objective photography; even satellite photos show the gaze of the governments and corporations that launched them.

In truth, whoever shares the image controls its context. Without careful consideration, quotation, and deployment, photographs—particularly in their reach toward even the most terrible beauty—dilute rather than elucidate meaning: "The aestheticizing tendency of photographs," as Sontag writes, "is such that the medium which conveys distress ends by neutralizing it. Cameras miniaturize experience, transform history into spectacle." Just as musculature, mountains, sunsets, voluptuous curves, and refracted light are made beautiful—part of our *natural* world—

so too is death, pain, war, starvation, isolation, and subjugation. Contemplated amorally and quoted unthinkingly, photography is beautification in the service of power, celebrating a hierarchy of suffering as an eternal verity of life on earth. It becomes one more way to say, as in photographs of dead or dying children: *This is how it is; nothing can be done.* Searching for truth in beauty alone elevates form over individuality. An aesthetics without ethics is a violent erasure.

This amoral approach to the beautiful is a terminal one. In "Fascinating Fascism," written alongside the essays that comprise *On Photography,* Sontag criticizes Nazi propagandist Leni Riefenstahl's photographs of the Nuba in southern Sudan—published nearly forty years after *Triumph of the Will*—as reflective of fascism's reductive, dehumanizing agenda. "What is distinctive about the fascist version of the old idea of the Noble Savage is its contempt for all that is reflective, critical, and pluralistic," she writes. Though the Nuba are Black and not Aryan, "Riefenstahl seems hardly to have modified the ideas of her Nazi films. And her portrait of the Nuba goes further than her films in evoking one aspect of the fascist ideal: a society in which women are merely breeders and helpers, excluded from all ceremonial functions, and present a threat to the integrity and strength of men." Here again: nature, eternal values, biological destiny; thinkers like Freud and writers like Paglia have prepared us to accept these as "common sense." Fascist and totalitarian movements promise this kind of hidden simplicity or universal translation—where animal nature prevails over cultural constructs, where what is meant to be is plucked from the chaos and brought to the fore. This is seductive because it erases contradiction, complexity, and hesitation, especially in increasingly complex, tolerant, and democratic environments. Thought becomes unnecessary. Speech—in images, in language, in art—requires no interpretation or interrogation. The inconsistencies that make us individuals cannot be tolerated. Fascism is pure form and we are destined to be shaped as its content, our lives superfluous.

***

For a nation that harbors such paranoia over the "thought control" deployed by totalitarian regimes depicted in our entertainment, both whiteness and male chauvinism (or toxic masculinity) seem peculiarly to alter one's beliefs and behaviors, consciously or not. But this is where representation becomes important: We grow more fluent in our identities as we familiarize ourselves with an image vocabulary that is larger than any one self could contain. As we see and share alternative, pluralistic versions of ourselves and of others, we resist a capitalist species of totalitarian control. But this resistance depends upon seeing—or watching.

On the day the *Esquire* story was published, Fielden defended himself from its critics, calling contemporary America a "Kafkaesque thought-police nightmare of paranoia and nausea, in which you might accidentally say what you really believe and get burned at the stake." A debate "used to be as important an ingredient of a memorable night out as what was served and who else was there. People sometimes even argued a position they might not have totally agreed with, partly for the thrilling intellectual exercise playing devil's advocate can be."

Later, Fielden alluded to "the digital Jacobins prepar[ing] the guillotine for me," referring to criticism from people who are not like Ryan (which also means, it should be noted, people who are not like Fielden), and who had spent the better part of two days articulating why the piece was so offensive, especially during Black History Month. That Fielden would equate critical dissent from Black Americans with public execution is hatefully irresponsible in a country where those same Americans are murdered without trials if they're even *perceived* to resist threats from police officers.

For many in this country, the continued valorization of a neutral, idealized whiteness—or of a standard way of being a man—brings literal death. When people say, *This hurts*, and Fielden responds with metaphors suggesting that he's the person at risk, he creates an equivalence so disingenuous you'd have a hard time believing it, at least if you were as insensitive to whiteness and misogyny as men like Fielden—or boys like Ryan—seem to be. But if you are white or cis-male or both, it is an ethical imperative for you to see these ideologies.

The consumption and creation of images, like the usage of language, are political; every choice has behind it an ethics. There was a time in my life, for example, when I filtered Black and brown men out of my porn. This "preference" did not enrich my life, but impoverished it. Most white gay men might not consider this act of selection to be toxic, but what could be more poisonous to an already vulnerable community? In adhering to my racially and bodily based type, I'd instructed myself that gay men are acceptable like this but not that. To me, gay meant white and young and fit and no one else—another imagined neutral that is anything but.

Some myths, Barthes said, are ancient: "But there are no eternal ones; for it is human history which converts reality into speech, and it alone rules the life and death of mythical language." As a historical imagination, assembled by human beings, myth is a theatrical vocabulary meant to help us understand, with great pleasure, the natural world. But taken as truth, it is—like Paglia's—a politics that erases its footsteps so as not to be followed or challenged. The myth of masculinity supposes men as aggressive, dominating, virile, and strong. Again, there's nothing wrong with loving these qualities in men or in oneself. But so too can one love and cherish the way men cry out in helpless frustration when denied their orgasms, or how they curl up and sleep like cats when their fingers and toes get too cold. Men too can be soft, carried around a room, penetrated, consoled when they cry, and objectified as beautiful bodies; and this too is masculine—this too finds joy in the emotional and physical experience of testosterone. One doesn't even have to be labeled male on one's birth certificate to assume and perform these traits.

In truth, masculinity is as welcome a performance as any other, but only in the safety of its theaters—never imposed upon others, and never as a mask the self feels it can't remove. Never, in a word, unsolicited.

"What we need is an angel," de Beauvoir said, "neither man nor woman—but where shall we find one?" There is a reason totalitarian frameworks reject, quarantine, and exterminate what is queer. Queerness is the ultimate protest against fascist binaries, including those established and enriched by capitalism. Capitalism too is a total philosophy, capable of assimilating anything measured against the rigidity of its definitions. Like fascism, it seeks to divide, classify, rank, and describe. This is, after all, how one assembles a product catalogue. When it comes to queerness, the capitalistic framework is particularly careful to police its images, showing consumers the cleanest, whitest, and least-threatening characters in advertisements and entertainment. It says, *Expressions of this behavior are allowed, but only as we've shown*. In Chomsky's metaphor, rather than reflect what is possible, capitalism "sets the bounds" for queer visibility and identity. Conversely, the celebration of gender fluidity, nonmonogamous relationships, bodies of every type, polyamory, communal households, pansexuality—even cosplay—are all acts of queer resistance; and not only against capitalistic predation but against any totalizing aesthetic mythography, Freudian or Marxist or Paglian or Hegelian or Smithian or otherwise. Queerness rejects absolutely the impulse to pin every butterfly to its board, place every specimen in its jar, and record every individual in the columns of its financial statements: profit or loss.

***

I was never supposed to write a book like this. Fiction was my landscape for imagining how to reconcile being a person; essays were for thinking. My nonfiction work was never supposed to be personal, in any sense of the word, and I was under no circumstances to use my sexuality as some kind of talking point. Neither was I supposed to refer, in interviews, to myself as a gay or queer writer. That part of me wasn't supposed to matter. I'd convinced myself that to be taken seriously as a writer I could be only an un-adjectived writer. But these two images were working to erase me, not help me. They were images the industry had chosen. My imagination had been what Sarah Schulman calls gentrified, a mentality "rooted in the belief that obedience to consumer identity over recognition of lived experience is actually normal, neutral, and value free." Just as, long ago, my assigned image of masculinity no longer fit (it's a hard suit to wear with a dick in your mouth), I came to see this image of the "neutral writer" as a straitjacket.

Yet there is no blank or neutral, not as a writer and not as a man. To aspire toward neutrality is to participate in your own oppression or diminution. For my part, growing up, I could at least look like Ryan (though I was shorter and, frankly, more handsome), but what does it mean for the American boys—trans, Black, femme, and so on—who can't even pretend to play the part? What they see on this magazine cover is pure exclusion: *This is the kind of boy who matters, and boys like you do not.* At the same time, the boys who do fit the mold—white, straight, and uninterested in the lives of others—are reminded that America loves them and will protect them at all costs, even if the price, for those other boys, is their lives.

What *Esquire* did was not "engage in debate," as Fielden claimed, but instead loudly shun concerns that queers, women, and people of color have raised for centuries—concerns especially pressing under the Trump administration. Editorially, it closed its eyes to reactionary whiteness and chauvinistic masculinity, regurgitating unchallenged narratives that pretend these harmful ideologies are neutral. By refusing to connect the dots between ignorance and systemic violence, *Esquire* actively policed who matters and who does not. It's the same wound pundits ripped open after the 2016 election, elevating and valorizing the suffering of white people rather than focusing on the deadlier, more widespread pain of marginalized persons. What *Esquire* upheld was the gentrification of American suffering, reiterating to its audience that pain and poverty and terror are irrelevant until they affect the white, the male, the straight, the Christian.

Only a few days before *Esquire* told us about the boy we already knew, a video of two very different boys had gone viral. A Black teenager is waiting outside a school. He's holding flowers and balloons. Another boy emerges from the building and rushes toward him. Other students cheer as they embrace, then kiss. It is a beautiful moment. Two boys are in love and their classmates celebrate it. It is also terribly sad: that was never me, and couldn't have been. There was no image I saw as a boy that convinced me it was possible.

A common lament is this country's obsession with "identity politics"—so phrased to make it seem as if the identities of marginalized persons are what's corroding our political discourse. For me, though, identity isn't about how I choose to approach politics; it's about how politics has approached me—or confined me, even attacked me. My sexuality isn't something I choose to think about every day; it is an identity assigned to me by an ignorance that threatens my life. This is an unsolicited politics. In return, it is ethical to demand that white people think of their own whiteness, that men see their masculinity as imposed from without. What we must demand—not only of editors but anyone who holds institutional or visible power—is to be aware of this ethics. The stories you choose, the words you leave on the page, and the images you frame are not games; the devil already has enough advocates. These choices—about magazine covers, about representation, about the images we come into contact with every moment of every day—are decisions that contribute to how livable my life in this country can be, not to mention the lives of millions I've never met. These are decisions that get people killed.

***

All of this is propaganda that can no longer be invisible. It's telling that totalitarianism, in America, is "unnatural." That fascism is unnatural. These are regimes, it is imagined, that restrict or deny freedom—to speak, to gather, to pray, even to think. We ground stories in these regimes because they fascinate us; we want to understand how human beings would allow such total control, not only over their lives but their imaginations. We want to imagine the circumstances under which people like me or like you, who might otherwise enjoy freedom, would accept such a narrow vision not only of what comprises a life, but of what is possible in a life.

It can't be said enough: Americans have no right to not understand those who allow themselves to be dominated by totalitarian rule. This nation—where freedom is merely a brand, an ideological export—is the most submissive, beaten, and terrified country on earth. This is a terror that's mounted for years, as Masha Gessen outlined in their essay "The Reichstag Fire Next Time." From Woodrow Wilson's Sedition Act of 1918—which criminalized "speech perceived as critical of or detrimental to the American war effort"—

to Roosevelt's internment of Japanese Americans to McCarthyism to the "secrecy, deceit, and paranoia of the Vietnam War years, which culminated in a president who had his opponents prosecuted and wire-tapped," the so-called "state of exception" of executive emergency powers throughout the twentieth century "came close to being the rule." What has changed since the September 11 terrorist attacks, which Gessen compares to the 1933 Reichstag fire in Berlin, is that "the enemy is not a nation or an army but a tactic, one that has existed for millennia. This war cannot be won, because a tactic cannot be eradicated. A war that cannot be won cannot end, and so it has not. Nor have the liberties surrendered by Americans in response to 9/11 been restored."

Any visit to an airport will illustrate just how thoroughly this nation is governed by fear—and not only from without but from within. As Arendt observes, "A fundamental difference between modern dictatorships and all other tyrannies of the past is that terror is no longer used as a means to exterminate and frighten opponents, but as an instrument to rule masses of people who are perfectly obedient." Primarily, Arendt is analyzing the rise and fall of the Reich and Stalin's rule in Soviet Russia, but reading her thoughts today offers an eerie, sickening, unsettling recognition: Americans have become the exhausted Germans, desperate for an easy way out of economic frustration; we have become the cowed Russians, too concerned with making it from here to there to protest our unconstitutional mistreatment. Remembering the immediate response to 9/11, Gessen notes that "Fear has a way of catapulting citizens into the inside of a lie ... Within hours of the September 11 attacks, 150 members of Congress gathered on the Capitol steps and sang 'God Bless America.' Some of them held hands. The strongest country on the planet was making a spectacle of fear and resolve." We have become the terrified Americans, so convinced by the sensibilities of entertainment—the terror and ecstasy of seeing a disaster we'd never seen before—that we behave as if something almost statistically impossible could happen to us at any moment, and therefore we must safeguard ourselves against it at all times, by any means. We became, as Gessen writes, mobilized:

> A key characteristic of the most frightening regimes of the past hundred years is mobilization. This is what distinguishes the merely authoritarian regimes from the totalitarian ones. Authoritarians prefer their subjects passive, tending to their private lives while the authoritarian and his cronies amass wealth and power. The totalitarian wants people out in the square; he craves their adulation and devotion, their willingness to fight and die for him ... A nation can be mobilized only if it knows its enemy and believes in its own peril.

This echoes Arendt's own observation of "the perpetual-motion mania of totalitarian movements which can remain in power only so long as they keep moving and set everything around them in motion ... If there is such a thing as a totalitarian personality or mentality, this extraordinary adaptability and absence of continuity are no doubt its outstanding characteristics."

Uncoincidentally, the fundamental, irreducible quality of capitalism—particularly America's brand of imperial capitalism—is motion: an aggressive, constant pursuit of novelty, innovation, and profit margins. Yet in the United States, capitalism is as natural as fascism is unnatural. Even if it is capitalism itself, as Russell indicates in his *History*, that has laid the groundwork for the fascist expression of totalitarianism:

> Though many still sincerely believe in human equality and theoretical democracy, the imagination of modern people is deeply affected by the pattern of social organization suggested by the

organization of industry in the nineteenth century, which is essentially undemocratic. On the one hand there are the captains of industry, and on the other the mass of workers. This disruption of democracy from within is not yet acknowledged by ordinary citizens in democratic countries, but it has been a preoccupation of most philosophers from Hegel onwards, and the sharp opposition which they discovered between the interests of the many and those of the few has found practical expression in Fascism.

This "imagination of modern people"—today, seventy years more modern than what Russell described—is visible even in the language we use in our day-to-day lives. Americans measure productivity not only at work but at home—whether we've done enough dishes or laundry, sent enough emails, texted enough friends, made enough plans. We talk about time management in our personal lives. We apologize for claiming sick time, for taking vacations. Instead of hobbies, we have side hustles, second-incomes, gigs. During the COVID-19 pandemic, article after article circulated advising us on how we could maximize our time in isolation. In place of the thought police Orwell imagined, Americans have created thought managers.

When she covered Adolf Eichmann's trial in Israel in 1961, Arendt was repulsed by this war criminal's tendency toward total banality:

> Officialese became his language because he was genuinely incapable of uttering a single sentence that was not a cliché . . . The longer one listened to him, the more obvious it became that his inability to speak was closely connected with an inability to *think*, namely, to think from the standpoint of somebody else. No communication was possible with him, not because he lied

but because he was surrounded by the most reliable of all safeguards against the words and the presence of others, and hence against reality as such.

Eichmann's envelopment in the vocabulary of his ideology, his subservience to it even at the level of language, illustrates the totalness of totalitarianism, that it is indeed within the power of a regime to limit what constitutes a life, as well as limit what one imagines is possible. Just suggest to a random American that we reduce the military, disarm or defund the police, pay people to stay home during a pandemic, and institute nationalized healthcare and free education to join the ranks of nearly all other Western nations. You will hear, most likely, how this is "not possible." Of course, this shouldn't be a surprise in a society where, to return to Arendt's words, there is "a way and philosophy of life so insistently and exclusively centered on the individual's success or failure in ruthless competition that a citizen's duties and responsibilities could only be felt to be a needless drain on his limited time and energy." We are too busy being productive, too involved in managing our time, to participate as citizens in our own democracy.

Accustomed as we are to entertainment, it's tempting to look for a mastermind giving the orders and signing the death warrants. Yet with most totalitarian structures, the movement outpaces its creators. As concerns the capitalist species of totalitarianism, the metaphor of evolution, or "natural selection," is more helpful. In nature, a species doesn't decide to evolve; it reacts, over time, to its environment. So too do individuals and systems respond to capitalist pressures, often involving competition, and change their behavior or rules or laws accordingly. Rather than subjects of some capitalist mastermind, we are evolving into totalitarian subjects via Capital Selection.

Rooted in an ideology predicated on expansion, acquisition, and unlimited growth at the expense of the entire world; establishing murderous regimes overseas in exchange for profit and national security; depriving other nations of their autonomy, wealth, and resources; branding itself as synonymous with freedom and liberty in the common imagination and warping our day-to-day language in the process; and of course having established itself upon two concurrent genocides, the United States of America's project of imperial capitalism is the most successful, longest lasting, most deeply entrenched, and—given the catastrophic threat of climate change—the deadliest of all totalitarian movements in world history; and it is not only still moving, but still accelerating.

*　*　*

Just as there's no unseeing the "toxic" aspects of masculinity or the horrific dynamics of whiteness once you've dragged them from their darknesses, so too is the capitalist imposition of identity vulnerable to light. Another of masculinity's epithets is "fragile"—an ideal way to describe the reactionary violence of men whose idea of masculinity is so easily threatened. It connotes a guarded notion of masculinity as immutable, as eternal. As, in other words, a relic. Frankly, a masculinity that can be called fragile is a masculinity that should be shattered; and so too should we imagine a fragile capitalism—something to shatter through identitarian experimentation, representation, and a plurality of contradictory, multifaceted images grounded in context. What we need is to resist the authority of unsolicited images.

Men are not monsters, but they do monstrous things wearing the masks of their culture's imposed masculinity. The average consumer—buying cheap products and bad art that undercut labor, skill, and creativity for the profit of a wealthy, corporate elite—does great harm to our culture and our planet indulging in interests they've been assigned or manipulated into cultivating. They, too, are not monsters. As with all repressive ideologies, it is the responsibility of the privileged to dismantle these systems—perhaps to great and disruptive pressure from those who are not privileged. A pretended neutrality is instead a complicity in imposing suffering on all individuals simply to protect a power structure. Believing or tolerating that "men are men" makes you nothing but a pawn. Believing or tolerating that what we see is what we've chosen—that a government whose primary concern is the protection and longevity of corporate wealth at the expense of the entire planet is the only electable option outside of Soviet Russia or Nazi Germany—makes you a pawn. Totalitarian systems rely on these pawns to destroy the minorities whose lives are inconsistent with the reductive myths they overlay onto reality, not to mention any imagined ideas that might alleviate or reverse this irresponsible, genocidal movement accelerating toward extinction.

There is no neutrality in visibility. There is no natural or eternal in how we, as modified creatures of technology and culture, live or die; and there are no ideologies or mythologies we can allow, any longer, to go on hiding in the dark.

II

WE HAVE ALWAYS WRITTEN WITH LIGHT

In one of Francesca Woodman's photographs, she's folded herself into a large curio cabinet but left the door ajar. Within the frame, we can see four of the cabinet's compartments. Woodman is in the lower right, her head leaning off the shelf, her hair draping onto the floor. Her feet are tucked into a corner, just behind the glass. In the compartment above her, also on the right, there are three plump waterfowl and a fox frozen in hunter's form, its teeth bared as it stares into a corner. All are dead, of course. To their left, a pair of some other kind of bird—limpkins, maybe, or egrets—stand delicately among sticks and feathers and dead leaves. Below them, directly left of Woodman herself, a taxidermy raccoon seems to have just stepped out of the darkness, its jaws open, its eyes locked on the nape of Woodman's neck. The photograph's locale—the floorboards, the dead things—indicate it was taken sometime in 1976, during her *Space²* series, in which she exhibits her blurred flesh in or nearby a large glass display case, sometimes with other models, sometimes with an unidentified skull.

Woodman's striking use of her body could align neatly with two contemporaries, Cindy Sherman and Robert Mapplethorpe, whose *Untitled Film Stills* and raw Polaroids of the 1970s were the famous beginnings of famously self-regarding careers. Yet in Woodman's work, her body is more object than subject. In fact, in many photographs, Woodman's skin appears to literally blur and blend into the wallpaper or the floorboards. Her use of bodies—her own and her models', whether displayed in a cabinet or hanging in a doorway—is surrealist: they could be furniture, décor, structural materials, toys, objets d'art, dead and stuffed creatures, sculptures, zoological specimens, or even living persons. In the surrealist imagination, there is no hierarchy of importance; everything is capable of registering the same interest or dismissal. The objects in Woodman's photographs, human and not, get spilled on by light; a rectangle from a window stretches across the floor, bisecting warped and wrinkled leaves of wallpaper that have curled onto the floorboards. A little pane of glass intensifies the light upon Woodman's fingers, visually slicing them at the knuckle. These objects, bodies included, remind us just how dramatically light can change a thing, how it bestows another side, another use, even another meaning. All objects are treated the same, given the same importance; all are worthy of, or deprived of, the gift of light. These are photographs "about" photography; they decrypt themselves.

In his journals, Hervé Guibert writes that the "most photographic" moment is often "but an event of light, without a subject." His own photographs, full of smoke and shrouds, filmy panes of glass, and overexposed nudes, are rich with these events, though not as surreal or claustrophobic as Woodman's tend to be. I've since realized that a lot of my favorite photographers—Woodman and Guibert included, but also Saul Leiter, Gueorgui Pinkhassov, Carrie Mae Weems, Peter Hujar, Nan Goldin, Trent Parke, and many others—seem to see the world in layers and tones of light rather than observable events, places, or persons (or, like André Kertész and Graciela Iturbide, in layers of shadow).

As Sontag remembers, her friend and mentor Joseph Brodsky said "there were two subjects: time and language." It's easy enough to understand how all photography is about time; if time is a river, photography flash-freezes the currents and chips them free, giving us petite and portable pieces of ice. But, like poetry, which sprays a kind of ink to make language visible—revealing its mutual tethers to reader and writer, speaker and hearer, showing how language attaches all of us to one another—certain photographs are not only about time, but about language.

If photography's relationship to time is what concerns me, its love of language, expressed by its most poetic photographers, is what enthralls me.

***

The literary interest in photography is a niche tradition. I came to it by chance, or a series of chances. Several years ago, I'd gone through a dry spell, unable to write anything for months. One day, I managed a few hundred words of something new. It felt momentous, and so—conditioned as I am like some horribly abused laboratory gerbil—I logged onto Twitter to celebrate. Since the era of being sincere or direct online ended sometime between 2010 and 2012, I couldn't just tweet "Finally working on something new!" so I searched for a gif—a moving image—from Tarantino's *Kill Bill*. At this point in the film, the Bride has just woken from her four-year coma and is trying to "will [her] limbs out of entropy [*sic*]." The gif I found is about three seconds long. The Bride's lips are moving. The camera gently approaches her face. The caption within the image reads, "Wiggle your big toe"—the actual dialogue Uma Thurman is reciting in this scene. When I posted it, I included my own additional caption—"re-learning how to write like"—which appeared just above this moving picture, as if a descriptive clause before a bulleted list. The nature of the gif is to repeat, and Thurman's lips move over and over; the camera pans in and snaps back like the lash of a whip; the captions—both the original and my own—never disappear. A viewer can linger as long as they like: this combination isn't going anywhere.

In the grammar of memes, the sentence was complete: "Re-learning how to write is like that scene in *Kill Bill* where the Bride wills her atrophied limbs back to life so she can walk and, ultimately, carry out her revenge." A few days later, when I'd finished a first draft, I followed up with another *Kill Bill* motion-grab: the Bride crossing the name "Vernita Green" from a page in a notebook called "Death List." I had, as they say, killed it.

As a novelist, I like to tell people that *Some Hell*'s inspiration came from a single gif—Laura Palmer, in *Fire Walk with Me*, waking up in the White Lodge and understanding what has happened to her. I suppose you can blame this book on Uma Thurman speaking to her foot.

Every once in a while, the structures of every day life—our habits, our consumptions, our ways of seeing and speaking—hit a bump, or they lurch and we feel their inertia, or a wheel lifts off the rails. Call it an out-of-capitalism experience; after spending so many minutes searching for images to put together a simple phrase—a phrase that is more efficiently stated in actual words—I saw what I'd done with the gif, and it fascinated me. I went out and bought my first Sontag books. At around this same time, one of my favorite novelists, Teju Cole, had just started writing about photography for *The New York Times* Magazine. Suddenly, I was *interested* in photography—especially the gif, a relative novelty.

If the primary characteristic of the photograph is stillness, the primary characteristic of the gif is motion. Developed in 1987 by CompuServe programmer Steve Wilhite, the graphics interchange format file is a multitude of images described over a fixed area. In the era of much slower modems, this meant that high-resolution images could be easily compressed and quickly transmitted. As usual, we can thank pornography for this innovation.

Today, the gif primarily provides a space for multiple images in a specific sequence, like frames in a strip of film. It expands the narrative possibilities of the still image by allowing looped animation. It doesn't freeze a moment so much as echo it, as a scratch on a record. Yet there's nothing cinematic, per se, about the gif. To experience cinema is to have its narrative unfold alongside you; the viewer becomes the film's contemporary. To experience a photograph or a gif produces a kind of relativity of seeing. No one glances at a photograph as it "occurred" in real time—that is, no one looks for a fraction of a second. As Cole observes in "The Image of Time": "Almost every photograph appears instantaneous. But of course, there's no such thing as 'instantaneous': All fragments of time have a length. In a photograph, the time during which the light is refracted by the lens, enters the aperture and is allowed to rest on the photosensitive surface could be 1/125th of a second, one-eighth of a second, half a second, a whole minute, much more or much less." When we stand before a photograph, it's this split second of exposure time that we see, repeated as long as we wish to look. The gif, whose repetition likewise repudiates the idea of real time, is just a longer version of the photograph.

Pairing gifs with previously unassociated captions is an expansion on the most elemental construction of the internet meme: image + caption. Often, the images are familiar (babies, puppies, screenshots from popular films or television shows, cats), and the captions equally so ("me trying to get my life together"; "when he asks if you're hungry"; "sorry to this man"). Both rotate through their possible permutations and both introduce new images or new captions as variants on the existing structure (pulling images from presidential debates or recent news stories, for example, and pairing with familiar, oft-used captions).

While the literary structure of the meme (juxtaposition) sinks its roots in metaphor itself, its continued transmission and propagation descend from metaphors of evolution. In his 1976 book *The*

Selfish Gene, Richard Dawkins observes that "we need a name for the new replicator, a noun that conveys the idea of a unit of cultural transmission, or a unit of *imitation*." The Greek-ish "mimeme" (from mimesis) would have done nicely, but Dawkins wanted "a monosyllable that sounds a bit like 'gene.'" Tying memes to genes was crucial to his metaphor: much like their biological antecedents, these cultural units would move from imagination to imagination and mutate or evolve along the way, independent of their "host's" intent or agency. While Dawkins disavows the adoption of "meme" for use in internet memes, one could argue that internet memes are culture's answer to genetic engineering, or at the very least meme husbandry. After all, there is no art (mimesis) that seeks to make an exact copy of life: there is always a deliberate mutation to make this piece of life visible, including introducing a boundary or a frame. Even at the level of metaphor, art never aims its arrow at exact imitation; its goal is to miss, but not so widely we don't hold our breath as it rushes by. To keep us on edge, its goal is to miss in a different way every time. It must mutate to remain delightful. To speed this up, we've become deliberate.

In a 2013 interview with *Wired*, Dawkins called the internet's usage of the meme a "hijacking" of his own term: rather than attempting an accurate copy, as genes do, internet memes are "deliberately altered" as they propagate themselves through culture. Each mutation now carries something of a signature.

The meme is a unit of language; it is also a unit of art. Like all units of language and most works of art, there's something chemical—and chemically finite—about memes. Their image + caption structure is the basic formula for how we've expressed ourselves for thousands of years. Memes—like jokes, like most works of art—aren't delightful for long. Like a science fair volcano's vinegar and baking soda, it first fizzes, then fizzles, its energy soon spent in circulation. It's a reaction anyone can begin and no one can undo. In the chemistry of language itself, words are metaphors that have long lost their spark. The fundamental units of language—tokens for irreducible concepts like *sun* or *cut* or *burn* or *die*—once gave breath to the ancient gods they inspired. Now, etymologists trace these particles back to their elemental origins, the rest of us left speaking in spent fuel.

Methods for transferring and disseminating information may evolve naturally from human interaction and reflection; they may also arise from deliberate mutation or violence. Linguistic conventions are often imposed by a ruling class, and dialects erased by war, disease, genocide, colonial oppression. In his *Course in General Linguistics*, Saussure dispelled with any nineteenth-century arrogance regarding linguistic teleology, prescriptive vocabularies, or stability: "All parts of [a] language are subject to change, and any period of time will see evolution of greater or smaller extent . . . The linguistic river never stops flowing." As this flow of language gathers momentum, "a kind of tacit convention emerges by which one of the existing dialects is selected as the vehicle for everything which is of interest to the nation as a whole." The consequence this has on society does not necessarily reflect anything inherent about the potential, nor the efficiency, of specific dialects or modes of communication; what is ultimately selected is simply what held out against the others.

> Not only can we see metaphor "fossilized" (as Emerson writes) in our modern linguistic compounds, but also traces of social struggle. "History does not merely touch on language," Adorno writes, "but takes place in it." There's a buried cardinality, a cartographic grammar of light and line, that shows how different ways of telling, of showing—of reading, of seeing—abrade one another, even reject one another. Language too is a history of violence.

As units of language, gifs and other commonly used meme images occupy a semiological middle space between image and abstraction. To play off Emerson's metaphor, memes are among the most unfossilized language units we see every day—a clear way, for those who can read them, to express oneself emotionally and intellectually, and yet still bubbling with energy; we can see them as language and as images simultaneously. In Saussure's terminology, gifs and other memes are a river that has not yet pulled us under—a language in the process of becoming. This would not have been possible without the twentieth century's elevation of photography as the ur-language of globalism (a cute word for imperial capitalism). If memes are becoming a language, photography became one decades ago—and with no lack of violence.

***

To access my social media, listen to music, check the weather, answer a text, look at porn, worry over my bank balance, read an email, or answer a call, I look carefully at my phone (sometimes bug-eyed) and wait for it to recognize me. When I sign up for a new service or website, I squint to decipher what's called a Captcha code, which is supposed to ensure that I'm not a robot (the frequency at which I'm wrong is troubling). My computer boops when I access a new app on my phone; my phone beeps when I log in to my email on a new computer. A few years ago, I was "verified" on Twitter: a blue checkmark proves I am the real Patrick Nathan.

Much like a digital photograph or darkroom print, the image of ourselves we wish others to see requires extensive manipulation of color, contrast, light, and shadow. We develop variations on our personality depending on who is viewing, and we call these individual prints personae. Meticulously constructed and carefully exhibited, our portfolio of personae questions the concept of authentication, valid only in light of its etymological root: we are indeed, as our facial signatures suggest, the author ("originator") of each and every one of these self-portraits.

A self-portrait is not its painter. An essay is not its author. These personae, these images of ourselves we call our selves, are only narratives. Filtered through the same algorithms and quoting a shared language of selfie poses, each projected self comes to resemble the others: we narrate ourselves based on the narratives we read in the images and personae of others.

Despite its technological aspirations toward documentation and preservation, photography has become simply one more way to tell a story.

As I write this, there are approximately 7.4 trillion photographs stored on hard drives and other digital devices. In 2021, humankind will take and upload another 1.4 trillion pictures. More than 75 percent of these photographs will be taken with mobile phones and shared on social media or some other public platform, where anyone will be able to save them, use them privately, modify them, repost them, and recirculate them.

Confronted with this daily tableau of images, the drive to make sense of them, to organize them, can be exhausting. Images are not so much looked at and copied as they are quoted. Whether plucked from social media feeds or archives, used in memes, or posted with simple and earnest captions ("me at the lake"), nearly all images are assigned meaning or provided context. The context for most consumers of images is simple: an expression of the producer's self.

We collect images as a way to remind ourselves of what matters to us, what is important, what we want to remember. Because one likes to believe in the story, in the consistency, of oneself. Unfortunately, our actions often don't mesh with our larger narrative. Events derail our plots. What was supposed to bring joy becomes a harbinger of anxiety, and ultimately of death.

"When we define the photograph as a motionless image," writes Barthes, "this does not mean only that the figures it represents do not move; it means that they do not *emerge*, do not *leave*: they are anesthetized and fastened down, like butterflies." Lovely to look at, but with a cost. "I allow myself to be photographed," Guibert writes—after Barthes—"not like someone who is still alive, but like someone who was still alive at the moment of the photograph."

We are back to that literary tradition I mentioned earlier— how language can reflect or interact with reality. That whole Plato thing. Years ago, fascinated by what I'd done with the gif and reading Sontag for the first time, I found an eerily familiar world in the 1970s of *On Photography*, her most important and, decades later, most contemporary book: "Ultimately, having an experience becomes identical with taking a photograph of it." Sontag connects the development of "fun" technology (Polaroids, Super 8s) with its application for self-surveillance. Photography "is a view of the world which denies interconnectedness, continuity." It is "atomized reality"—moments outside of time, and therefore outside understanding: "As Brecht points out, a photograph of the Krupp works [a German munitions factory] reveals virtually nothing about that organization. Understanding is based on how [something] functions. And functioning takes place in time, and must be explained in time. Only that which narrates can make us understand." Photography is a surrealist ethos, a democratization of nouns: "It is photography that has best shown how to juxtapose the sewing machine and the umbrella, whose fortuitous encounter was hailed by a great Surrealist poet [Lautréamont] as an epitome of the beautiful." So flattened, the juxtaposed objects lose their accents, their stress. Photography, as a democratization of seeing—giving equal attention and compassion to a burn victim and the shadow beneath a park bench—empties subjects of their meanings. Images are presented without context,

In her early essay on happenings, Sontag reflected on the isolating tendency of surrealism, how it "stresses the extremes of disrelation—which is preeminently the subject of comedy, as 'relatedness' is the subject and source of tragedy."

without "time" before and after to understand. So isolated, they do not narrate. There is no reference point for meaning.

Capitalism, Sontag writes, "requires a culture based on images. It needs to furnish vast amounts of entertainment in order to stimulate buying and anesthetize the injuries of class, race, and sex." In place of social change, we get "a change in images. The freedom to consume a plurality of images and goods is equated with freedom itself," which reduces "free political choice" to "free economic consumption." Reading *On Photography* today is important not merely because we're collectively hoarding trillions of photographs, but because our primary day-to-day experience with one another as human beings has been shattered into an ongoing incoherence of images.

Social media is a surrealistic environment that juxtaposes photographs of dying children against a snarky Wendy's advertisement, a racist remark from the president against a friend who wants a book recommendation. This sensibility of flatness, of sameness, is what enables the form of social media—a frame of advertisements CF. P45 in need of constant content. Because of the financial incentives built into the framework itself, the only thing that matters about an image on social media is that we see it.

Politically, photography has long flirted with the illusion that taking and distributing an image is liberating, even universal. If people see, the story goes, they will understand. This too is surreal. Today one sees this same assumption in videos of murders, photographs of incredible violence, or even footage of the president saying something terrible he thought would pass in private— with these horrors exposed, they will certainly "change hearts and minds." *This happened*, a photograph says. *This is real*. But, Sontag goes on, "the photographer's insistence that everything is real also implies that the real is not enough. By proclaiming a fundamental discontent with reality, Surrealism bespeaks a posture of alienation which has now become a general attitude in those parts of the world which are politically powerful, industrialized, and camera-wielding." Rather than change, alleviate, or eliminate the suffering or strangeness of others, Sontag suspects that photography has only enabled the planet's privileged societies to collect the sufferings or strangenesses of others: photography as visual colonialism.

***

None of this is possible without photography's first and most important promise. Writing a letter in 1843, Elizabeth Barrett "long[ed] to have such a memorial of every being dear to me in the world. It is not merely the likeness which is precious in such cases—but the association and the sense of nearness involved in the thing . . . the fact of the *very shadow of the person* lying there fixed forever!" With the daguerreotype and the photograph, what was or would be gone could now be taken with you, saved from the corrosive accumulation of years and the unreliability of memory. Perhaps photography, as a technology and a medium, is haunted by death because it tried, arrogantly, to refute death's claim on memory.

Though of course, as Guibert observes, there is a tendency for certain photographs to "quickly turn yellow and crack around the edges whenever they're exposed to light or handled too often (after a while, light always revenges itself for having been taken prisoner—it gathers itself back)."

With this refutation of death is an assumption or declaration of accuracy, of exactness. Daguerre's invention was "not merely an instrument which serves to draw nature," he told his investors, but a way to give nature "the power to reproduce herself." Not only can an image of a thing live forever, but its image can live faithfully. Despite nearly two centuries of manipulation, staged photographs, alterations, "deep fakes," and other infidelities entwined with photography since its inception, there remains the naïve assumption, so easily disprovable, that what we see in a photograph is somehow true, or at the very least truer than what is remembered or narrated.

At the time I am writing this, a search for the #nofilter hashtag on Instagram returns 266,415,808 images. Many are landscapes. Some are close-ups of flowers, trees, or handfuls of beach sand. Few are selfies. Most are sunsets, an event that occurs every day on earth. In the standard sunset photograph—a genre of its own—the horizon is centered vertically, an equal field of murky land or water below a mirrored quantity of murky sky, and that brilliant wound of color scratched through the middle. It's the color, I think, that people find so hard to believe, and what they ask us, through their photographs, to believe along with them. What #nofilter promises, ostensibly, is true colors, or verified colors. *This happened* we understand when we see #nofilter; or, in a more familiar phrase: *This is a true story*—a desperation particularly apt for the least realistic, least honest, least literary, and most photo-centric of all platforms.

Of course, even those real sunsets are filtered. The scene's selection as a photograph, as well as its frame—the edge of what we see—create a narrative of boundaries: *this* is what was seen, and *that* is whatever wasn't photographed. All photographers make decisions. "Every time we look at a photograph," writes John Berger in *Ways of Seeing*, "we are aware, however slightly, of the photographer selecting that sight from an infinity of other possible sights." Not only is something taken into the future, but everything else is left behind—this is the grammar of the photograph's frame. The ubiquity of #nofilter exposes the preserved moment for the idyllic lie that it is: an artful re-creation. Similarly, its very deployment—going out of one's way to promise that this, right here, is a faithful token of reality—contaminates the image with an expression of selfhood; it tells the viewer the story of just how badly the photographer wants to be believed.

Instagram, as a social phenomenon, not only betrays the photographic desire for fidelity, but its unique braiding of fascination with anxiety in capturing moments in time. With an increasing variety of filters and aspect ratios, Instagram's daily upload of ninety-five million images preserves and remembers ninety-five million different moments in the lives of over a billion active users. When launched in 2010, Instagram's only aspect ratio was a perfect square, similar to the Polaroid and Kodak Instamatic formats of the 1970s. In 2016, the design collective Canva found that, after Clarendon ("an all-purpose filter that brightens, highlights, and intensifies shadows for color that pops"), the most popular Instagram filter is Gingham: "a nostalgic choice. Once reserved for videos, this vintage-inspired photo filter lets Instagram users evoke the past."

Outside of Instagram, photography's fetishistic relationship with the past is just as prevalent. In one professional photograph, we see a Spanish Gothic cinema house, its frescoes dripping from the ceiling, the intricate carvings that frame the screen crumbling onto the floor. In another, someone's abandoned apartment, the kitchen cupboards leaning on their countertops, a small unsmashed television resting on a cheerless laminate table. The walls look as if they could be violated. In other images, warped mansions sink into overgrowth; a shattered greenhouse becomes a garden's mausoleum.

The sensibility of decay is nothing new, but in Yves Marchand's photographs of Detroit and in Matthew Christopher's *Abandoned America* series—particularly in their widespread presence on Tumblr and Pinterest—we talk about these photographs as a new genre: ruin porn. But as Sontag writes, the photographer Clarence John Laughlin was summoning ghosts in the 1930s with his pictures of "decaying plantation houses of the lower Mississippi, funerary monuments in Louisiana's swamp burial grounds, Victorian interiors in Milwaukee and Chicago." As an endeavor in "extreme romanticism," Laughlin's work hints, too, at a form of "relic making." There is nothing scientific, Sontag says, about the American photographer's ongoing project of documentation. Photography's effectiveness "depends on its steadily enlarging the familiar iconography of mystery, mortality, transience"; however, this "mournful vision of loss" comes to warp our vision of the past so severely that it reverberates all the way into the present, into this very moment. Photography "offers instant romanticism about the present. In America, the photographer is not simply the person who records the past but the one who invents it." To snap a photo is to instantaneously condemn a thing, even a person, to what is no longer.

In 2004, the E! network launched *The Soup*, a half-hour recap of pop culture events from the previous week. A harbinger of "In Case You Missed It" clip-based media consumption, *The Soup* managed to portray last week as though an era long past, worthy of nostalgia. Fawning over moments, a lot of what might have escaped notice became enshrined in pop culture (including, most famously, Whitney Houston shouting "kiss my ass" at Bobby Brown). *The Soup* created content out of other networks' content—a proto-meme sensibility.

In October 2015—only two months before *The Soup* went off the air—Twitter launched its "Moments" feature, a customizable tab that functions as a newsfeed or collection of current events, including awards ceremonies, noteworthy deaths, album releases, political news, or les scandales du jour. Unlike Twitter's list of trending topics,

A recurring complaint on social media is the relentless flood of news (time) and the wish to escape it (death). The drive to narrate, to make meaning, is obfuscated by sheer volume. It's no wonder, as Sebald writes, that Barthes saw in the "man with a camera an agent of death." In our consumption of images, each moment ebbs away like a drop of blood dripped from our veins into a vial, frozen for some future study.

these moments do not appear as an ongoing, constant stream of tagged tweets about a unifying event. Instead, a Moment appears as a clean, easy-to-read headline with a brief explanation and a large, professionally shot accompanying image, much as one would see on a news website. Twitter encourages you to tweet about this moment and share it with your followers, which wouldn't be so troubling if most of these moments did not appear from verified (read: official, authoritative, organized, corporate) sources. These moments are sponsored snapshots of information events. At any given time of day, opening the tab is akin to perusing an online photo album: we flip through these images of culture and select what we wish to spend more time studying, more time internalizing, more time remembering. *Just look at everything that happened today*, one might sigh, marveling at how much simpler life was at seven o'clock that morning before the world continued to complicate itself. Every day, we are invited to see how information ruins our innocence.

On a personal level, Twitter extends this capability for the creation and curation of moments in its users individual lives. This seems like Twitter's version of Facebook's ambiguous "life event." On both platforms, users have the ability to author and publish the moments in their timelines that they wish followers or visitors to notice, to see before all others. *This*, our moments say, *is what I want you to know and remember about me.* Displayed as they are on our timelines or profiles, these moments become—like their less personal counterparts of cultural information—images in and of themselves. These once dynamic parts of our lives, lived out in time, lie down flat and become tradable, consumable, sharable, and—of course—deletable. Like the cultural prescriptive memory that encourages us to never forget Matthew Shepard or 9/11, our personal galleries of life-images—our individually curated histories—demand that visitors, be they friends or strangers, never forget the sponsored self we believe (or wish) ourselves to be. In many articles targeted toward Instagrammers, users are advised to keep a close eye on the look of their profile—if the tiles of images complement or clash, if they flow like an elegant fabric or overwhelm like some grandmother's hideously patched quilt. An aesthetically pleasing history will, it is assumed, invite more followers.

Cantilevered opposite these aestheticized personal pasts, of course, are equally fussed-over futures. Up until recently, the most common form of images most people in capitalist nations came across every day were advertisements. Berger, in *Ways of Seeing*, calls them "publicity images," which "must be continually renewed and made up-to-date." Yet as saturated as we are by advertisements, "they never speak of the present. Often they refer to the past and they always speak of the future." Just as a photograph entombs a moment of time and clips the past from the present, the publicity image, Berger says, "is always about the future buyer. It offers him an image of himself made glamorous by the product or opportunity it is trying to sell. The image then makes him envious of himself *as he might be*" (emphasis mine). In a consumerist culture, we curate the images that excite our desire to spend money to become someone else, even if it's only our past self we sentence to envying who we may become.

Berger's ideas center upon literal, paid advertisements (*Ways of Seeing* was published in 1972), by which he meant magazine ads, television commercials, radio jingles, billboards, product packaging, etc. There was no social media, strictly speaking, in the seventies. However, he does mention a personal custom that anticipates certain platforms:

Adults and children sometimes have boards in their bedrooms
or living-rooms on which they pin pieces of paper: letters, snap-

shots, reproductions of paintings, newspaper cuttings, original drawings, postcards. On each board all the images belong to the same language and are all more or less equal within it, because they have been chosen in a highly personal way to match and express the experience of the room's inhabitant.

If this sounds like Pinterest, Tumblr, or Instagram, it should: it serves a similar purpose. Before the internet, we collected these images, cultural and personal, as a way to remind ourselves of what matters to us, what is important, what we want to remember. In office cubicles, employees still hang calendars full of photographs of landscapes, of cities they've never visited; at home, a newspaper clipping on the fridge might remind us of a vacation we'd like to take, a book we'd like to read. Surrounding oneself with images is a form of aspiration; just as we define our lives by the gallery we curate of past images, we survive on the breath of our future selves, what we might become. Introducing this concept to social media, where a following can witness our aspirations in aggregate (scrolling through our tableau of desires) or in real time (liking and sharing these images as we post them), is a way of broadcasting our own personal publicity campaigns: *this is what I'd like to be.*

Naturally, just as we tend to learn from and copy one another in our methods of curating, even policing, our images of the past, so too do our public aspirations—our vision boards—cross-contaminate and homogenize desire. A friend or stranger might share a photograph of some country cottage, a fire kindled in a large stone hearth, a book spine-up on the arm of a chair, a cup of coffee on a side table with one hyper-contrasted curl of steam; until now, you might have thought your ideal life would be spent at the beach or in a Parisian apartment, but now this cottage, and others like it, could become a lifestyle to chase. Reproductions of works of art shared to social media timelines become advertisements for styles of life: *I wish I was as cultured, as familiar with art, as you*, or *I wish I traveled to faraway museums as often as you*. Even the image of a Facebook friend—one you might well have seen in person yesterday—getting dinner at a restaurant becomes an image of publicity: the glamour of wanting an experience you aren't having, not to mention the little kernel of consumerist shame that you weren't asked, that you weren't good enough, to join.

In short, we have learned to present ourselves as images, to see one another as images. On social media—the primary method by which most people in capitalist nations experience one another every day—we are discontinuous with ourselves and with others; our friends resemble a catalogue of images to consume, reject, or discard. As images, any pretense of meaning vanishes from our lives. Crushed between the immense visibility of an aesthetically pleasing, deeply curated past and future, the present is becoming an infinitesimally smaller and smaller moment in time, and yet here, in this virtual blink of an eye, is the entire weight of our agency as human beings. We are holding our individual wills in a container of time almost impossible to perceive, impossibly small. No wonder Barthes—and Guibert, and Henri Cartier-Bresson, and Diane Arbus and so many others—saw, in such seeing, so much death.

***

In this capitalism-of-seeing, confined to near immobility between past and future, we rob ourselves of the consciousness that human beings exist continuously in time, and that our beliefs, opinions, desires, and deeds shift accordingly. The photographic ethos encourages a split—that whoever or whatever we're seeing is somehow separate from us; but in a world where anyone can be transformed

At the close of *On Photography*, Sontag conjures the metaphor of conservation: "If there can be a better way for the real world to include the one of images, it will require an ecology not only of real things but of images as well." Azoulay answers Sontag's call by changing the verb. To *watch* invokes a lapse of time. It is to accept that every image of a person you encounter, no matter how flat or reduced or airbrushed, is or was another human being existing in time, complete with aspirations, faults, guilt, talents, loneliness, and terror.

into an image, there is no split: we are all the image *and* its spectator, and we owe it to one another to be watchful.

Photography is a technology—which is to say, it's not a weapon. It's not, in a strict sense, Barthes's "agent of death," even if it does trade in images of death. Even if it does promise, in some way, to bring something of its subjects into a time they cannot follow. Photography is hardly the first technology to promise transcending the boundaries of one's own life—of reaching beyond the "brief crack of light," as Nabokov called it, "between two eternities of darkness"—and, of course, hardly the last. Yet there remains something about it that most of us, including those who surveil themselves with thousands of photographs every year, are unable to see.

In her essay "Kim Kardashian West Is the Outsider Artist America Deserves," Laura Jean Moore describes how female self-portraiture "upends historical norms of female representation and power, and places the power of depiction squarely in the hands of the subject." In assuming herself and her life as a subject, "Kardashian West is part of an established legacy of female artists and writers who have created art from the realm of the intensely personal and confessional." Via Instagram, Kardashian West narrates her self in carefully selected images with total artistic agency. Her story is one of empowerment, beauty, and—strangely enough, via a distortion of the self—self-acceptance. (Naturally, she rarely mentions the immense, uncirculated stockpile of wealth and resources that enable such self-acceptance, nor how much capital and labor is expended by her and her employees to arrive at such selfies.)

Kardashian West's photographic project seems an inversion of

Cindy Sherman's, who has long suppressed the personal and the confessional despite her physical body being the subject of almost all her work. In "A Piece of the Action: Images of 'Woman' in the Photography of Cindy Sherman," Judith Williamson argues that Sherman adapts the traditional uses of women in art, journalism, and advertising as divining rods for dominant societal narratives: "An image of a woman's face in tears will be used by a paper or a magazine to show by *impression* the tragedy of war, or the intensity of, say, a wedding. From the face we are supposed to read the emotions in the event." In Sherman's *Film Stills* project, Williamson says, "the very reference to film invites this interpretation. Film stills are by definition a moment in a narrative. In every still, the woman

In *Fetishism and Curiosity*, Laura Mulvey suggests that each of Sherman's images is "a cutout, a tableau suggesting and denying the presence of a story ... The *Film Stills* parody the stillness of the photograph and they ironically enact the poignancy of a 'frozen moment.' The women in the photographs are almost always in stasis, halted by something more than photography."

suggests something other than herself, she is never complete: a narrative has to be evoked." Instead of highlighting how narrative can imbue a self with agency, Sherman's oblique personae are deprived of agency. The women in her photographs are victims of narrative, used in someone else's story.

So how do we watch a photograph that is subverting the invitation to watch?—that is predicated on our desire to find a narrative, and to thwart it? In a 1983 interview with *American Photographer*, Sherman observed the uncanny confusion many felt in experiencing her work: "Some people have told me they remember the film that one of my images is derived from, but in fact I had no film in mind at all." Sherman's *Film Stills*, perhaps more than any other photographic series, illustrates the temptation to project a narrative upon an image. As a consequence, it reveals, too, just how easy it is to lose oneself in that image—to erase oneself with a story that isn't your own.

Sherman, like some of the best artists working with the medium of photography, reveals to us how the desire to make meaning can often eclipse the truth, and how reality, inconsistent and

CF. P56 abrasively random, gets lacquered over with fiction.

***

Meaning—or narrative—isn't always what we see, or even look for, in images. In 1868, following the International Exposition in Paris, the Italian novelist and essayist Vittorio Imbriani published "La quinta promotrice," a collection of his observations and theories on contemporary European art. This included his theory of the *macchia*, which Teju Cole describes as "the total compositional and coloristic effect of an image in the split second before the eye begins to parse it for meaning." Approaching a painting, one is most likely to see before anything else its arrangement of colors, shapes, shadows, and space, and only afterward begin to understand those colors as flesh or flora, those shapes as human, or as stone. This visual macchia ("stain") acts, Imbriani says, upon the nerves before the consciousness can interpret it; like anything primal, it readies the human animal before the human being. "Imbriani's was an argument for the inner life of pictorial effect," Cole writes, "not so much about the way in which visual organization transcended subject matter but the way in which it preceded subject matter." This seems to embrace Impressionism down to its most subconscious, emotional level—one's passions excited prior to understanding, which Edmund Burke described as the sublime.

Cole—a photographer as well as a writer—describes experiencing something similar when he uses Google's "Search by Image" function to find "visually similar images" to his own work. What he found, he wrote, "told me what I knew but hadn't articulated about the pictorial idea of my own picture, its rhetoric of red and shadow and scatter. It was like hearing a familiar tune played on unfamiliar instruments, with dramatic changes in the timbre but the pitches staying the same."

Attempting this same experiment with gifs instead of still images, Google doesn't return visually similar images but instead images that are contextually similar: gifs or stills from the same films, for example, or the same moments in culture. But that is not to say a macchia of motion does not exist. There are gifs that echo other gifs in their variations of movement, their choreography, as in Tumblr gif sets that assemble tapestries of images. They are synchronous, separate but simultaneously so.

Unlike sets of gifs that recount jokes in multiple frames, the viewer doesn't read these choreographed gifs sequentially, but opens their eyes to a quilt of motion. The delight here is in the moment before the brain can see each gif individually, before it can understand. Even porn gif sets offer a macchia of

Toward the end of his life, Guibert wrote in his journal that he "dreamt several times, recently, of the existence of a type of photograph that overflows in its restitution of the instant it has captured, a little like the cinema, but rather like a sort of temporal, transparent holograph."

flesh that echo the ecstasy, and the anachronisms, of the erotic moment. They reveal the beauty of motion in sex; their emotional stain is one of rhythmic synchronicity, of bodies transcending understanding. Even a captured cumshot—that curtain call of the video clip—is here presented as infinite, a fantasia in which pleasure can flow in perpetuity. Any narrative beyond the body's becomes inconsequential.

The gif's unique macchia of motion is what makes it valuable as a unit of language, especially as used in memes. Moving there in the frame is an array of colors, a pacing of movement, and a unique, repeated choreography; and all of this our nerves register before, first: understanding what's literally taking place in the image; second: reading the caption that's been assigned to it; and third: completing the juxtapositional association so we can perceive what the meme is trying to say. In short, our eyes soak up the gif's stain of motion before we even perceive that someone is trying to communicate with us: the impression precedes language.

Gif-based memes, like all memes, risk entering our everyday usage; read often enough, they become part of our standardized vocabulary of motion. As Britney Summit-Gil observed in her essay "Gif Horse," there are ancillary technologies cropping up all the time meant to augment the technology of the gif as language: "Sharing a gif now has been streamlined and democratized by the rise of searchable databases like Giphy and by the integration of gifs into phone apps. Finding just the right clumsy puppy or celebrity eye-roll is as easy as finding the right word in the moment, making communicating through gifs commonplace." Proliferating as they are across multiple platforms of text-based communication, the risk of unique gifs cementing themselves as specific connotations, and one day denotations, increases exponentially. Lauren Michele Jackson, for example, has written about how gif search engines can create clichés of motion, even racial slurs of motion. Discussing the commonplace deployment of "black reaction gifs" by white users, Jackson describes how "these are the kinds of gifs liable to come up with a generic search like 'funny black kid gif' or 'black lady gif.' For the latter search, Giphy offers several additional suggestions, such as 'Sassy Black Lady,' 'Angry Black Lady,' and 'Black Fat Lady' to assist users in narrowing down their search." This kind of "digital blackface" is a consequence of a delightful linguistic technology left unexamined and uncriticized—sort of like able-bodied persons continu-

Put another way, digital blackface is what happens when metaphor is cleaved from ethics and from politics, consigned solely to aesthetics.

ing to refer to themselves or others as "paralyzed with fear," as "tone deaf."

Of course, a shared vocabulary of motion preceded the widespread use, or even the invention, of the internet. Since the 1950s, communities of gay men have quoted not only the dialogue of camp films, but the motions as well—Anne Baxter's hand gestures in *The Ten Commandments* or Bette Davis's shoulder shrugs in *All About Eve* (or really, *anything* from *All About Eve*). For decades now, covens of young people have quoted, in speech and in gesture, every frame of *Monty Python and the Holy Grail* or *The Rocky Horror Picture Show* from memory. What has changed with the internet is our ability to quote motion in writing.

Via gif-based memes, our person-to-person language of motion is gaining a writing system, and with it an increasing tendency toward standardized meanings. Like the photograph, which clips a moment out of time and uses it to say *this is how things looked in this moment*, the gif has captured how it was that we moved in that moment. It liberates motion itself from time and elevates it to a mythology of movement; and it's in this technological middle space where we find ourselves, right now, able to write this captured motion but simultaneously experience it as art. It hasn't yet fossilized, not completely, into language.

The cliché—or the dead metaphor, or the image we see instead of watch, or the gif we read instead of enjoy—is where art ends. It is, after all, a kind of death—not for the person but for

In *Crowds and Power*, Canetti distinguishes the crowd, which is fixed and "centripetal" in its force, from the pack, which is "a unit of *action*." Packs, too, have a tendency to shift identities; a pack of hunters becomes a pack of mourners if one of their kind is killed in the hunt. "Some of these transmutations," he writes, "have been taken out of their wider context and *fixed*. They have acquired a special significance and become rituals." This is an attempt to catch or control a transformation, to capture change itself. The gif could be, in Canetti's vocabulary, a shared ritual belonging to a pack of individuals.

what persons create—and what we see in these corpses is where language begins; and from there it's the new metaphors, the next images, the future works of art, that we build from these bones.

The technological solution called forth by photography and later mutated into film, television, video, computer animations, succeeded so profoundly that it has become the medium in which we live, but it is only a medium of flickering light and darkness.

—REBECCA SOLNIT,
River of Shadows

In his memoirs of his famous father, filmmaker Jean Renoir recalls, as much as he can, the moment French Impressionism found its way into the world. Auguste Renoir and his peers—Monet, Cézanne, Pissarro, Sisley, Bazille—had taken a few rooms at Marlotte, near the forest of Fontainebleau. It was there, Renoir writes, "that they were, in Monet's phrase, 'to ensnare the light, and throw it directly on the canvas' . . . Behind the facile effects of rays of light shifting down from the foliage they discovered the essence of light itself." The painter Renoir, his son says, was particular about light, going so far as to refuse to paint by artificial light of any kind. That Impressionism is contemporaneous with the earliest days of photography—and that photography was immediately democratized as a public technology "for all of France"—hints at a nascent consciousness of light.

Upon the plates of the photographers, light falls; upon the canvases of the painters, light moves. If capturing the way light fell or flickered is our technology for carrying these visions around with us and for sharing them with others, the way we read these visions is another, much older technology—our first technology.

***

According to Google Maps, Mount Ida is a twenty-nine-hour walk from the ruins of Troy. These days, the route hugs country roads that cut through farmland and the occasional village, at least until the foothills, where—satellites show—you see mostly trees, escarpments of pale rock and red dirt, cell towers, lens flares. There's a turn toward the southern coast of Çanakkale, and then through the resort city of Altinoluk. The approach to Ida is from the southeast, back into the foothills and up to its modest summit—just over a mile above sea level. From there, one can see, in the distance, the hill where the city burned, the beach where the Achaeans camped. I've never been there, but I can look any time I wish.

Three thousand years ago, the route was more direct. In one version of the story, Helen makes the journey to beg Paris's first wife, Oenone, to heal his battle wounds. In another version, it is Paris himself who crosses the plains, only to die on the mountainside. Despite the road signs and farm fences, it's easy to picture Helen fraught with worry as she hurries through fields of wheat, or Paris bleeding on the peasants' crops as he crawls toward the woman he abandoned. From this perspective—soaring over Asia Minor or, through the uploaded photos of tourists and travelers, gazing out over the crumbled walls of Troy—one is free to drop in and out of the city without limitation, to travel from the plains of Ilium to Mount Ida with a click. Like other, more ancient surveilling eyes, one can observe without the burden of being. All these years later, one can look at Troy through the same lens as the gods.

There is a moment, as Roberto Calasso puts it, "in which the peculiarly Greek breaks away from the Asian continent . . . That moment is the Greek discovery of an outline, of a new sharpness, a clean, dry daylight. It is the moment when man enters into Zeus, into the clear light of noon." This, and not so much godly or "of a god," is perhaps what Homer meant when he called his heroes divine (*dîos*): "the clarity, the splendor that is always with them and against which they stand out." This light, for them, is crucial—a spotlight beneath which we see them live out their lives. It is, too, because of that light that darkness is knowable, that the threat of it is visible: "All the more irresistible then must one's brief spell in the light have appeared," against which our death looms—"an unparalleled cruelty."

Fittingly, Zeus ("to shine") may be the god to whom more words owe their lineage than any other: day, diurnal, divine, daily, diary, deity, diva, providence, journal, journey, dismal, diet, meridian, adjourn, circadian, quotidian, dial, clear, clarity, psychedelic, July, jovial, Tuesday, deus, sky, heaven. He fathered the day and all its variants, by which we see and measure our actions.

Clicking and dragging across the Aegean, tracing Agamemnon's return to Mycenae, it's easy to evoke another divine image: God hovering over the face of the waters, before the division of light from darkness. Above the Mycenaean ruins, just north of modern Argos, satellites show the citadel as distinct from the hillside. Here—less remote, and within a country famous for its ruins—there are far more uploaded photographs than at Troy. The great stone lions at the gate, the circles of graves, the view of the rolling hills from which a conquering general who may or may not have called himself Agamemnon surveyed his kingdom just after he'd destroyed another: one Google user has given the archaeological destination three out of five stars.

During the research process for what would become her novel *Cassandra*, Christa Wolf projected herself into the future. In the early 1980s, traveling across Greece, Crete, and Turkey, she wonders, "What kind of faith will the people of the future (assuming there *are* people in the future) read out of our stone, steel, and concrete ruins?" If we're to take history as a reliable measure, the story of the twentieth and twenty-first centuries will, in two or three thousand years, be quite reduced: we built the freeways because we thought they would save us; we lost our great coastal cities out of hubris; we destabilized an entire subcontinent to defend something called freedom. Every ruin has its myth; every war has its Helen. Like memory itself, history is an act of erasure and re-creation, a replacement of the past with an image of the past: a memorial, say, that "honors" those who were slain, or a foundation that "fights homophobia." This is elemental in Wolf's work: "There is and there can be no poetics which prevents the living experience of countless perceiving subjects from being killed and buried in art objects." Art, all too often, is the trophy cut from the corpse of its muse.

***

Writing for *Harper's* in 2014, Rebecca Solnit outlined Cassandra's modern predicament, lamenting the failure of our collective imaginations to enshrine her as we have Helen, Achilles, Odysseus, Paris, Agamemnon. "Generations of women," Solnit wrote, "have been told they are delusional, confused, manipulative, malicious, conspiratorial, congenitally dishonest, often all at once. Part of what interests me is the impulse to dismiss and how often it slides into the very incoherence or hysteria of which women are routinely accused." This suppression or denial of truth—particularly in regard to sexual assault and harassment—would indicate that Cassandra is the perfect character through which we can see, understand, and undermine contemporary misogyny. She offers the potential to narrate misogyny. But being ignored was always her pain. To impress her, Apollo bestowed her the gift of prophecy. However, when she refused sex with the god, he cursed her: she and her prophecies would never be believed. Even in the *Oresteia*, her voice goes unheard. "I say you will see Agamemnon dead," she warns Aeschylus's chorus, now a slave in the Mycenaean court—standing, perhaps, before those same lions tourists have photographed for decades. The chorus only hushes her, making way for Agamemnon's death—not to mention her own.

In Wolf's novel, Cassandra is a brilliant, wise, and deductive young woman, far too reasonable to get swept up in so foolish a war. Her so-called madness is her burden of being Troy's sole moral compass, the only person who questions authority. "A judgment had been passed on me," she says, "but how could I be guilty when I had done nothing but tell the truth?" It is exactly this truth that makes Wolf's novel such a sad, chilling portrayal of war—and of rape: no one ever wants the truth, and may openly, even violently, refuse it.

Cassandra warns Priam, her father and her king, not only of the war's outcome but the effects of war itself: "The first sign of war: We were letting the enemy govern our behavior." The answer she receives is both unsurprising and crushingly modern: "Priam explained to me that in war everything that would apply in peace was rescinded." Yet *war* isn't even the term the Trojans are permitted to use: "Linguistic relations prescribed that, correctly speaking, it be called a 'surprise attack.' For which, strange to say, we were not in the least prepared." Vocabulary is crucial in Priam's defense. When Menelaus, Helen's husband and Agamemnon's brother, is seated at the head of a banquet table with Priam and Hecuba, the court is forbidden to refer to him with the traditional term, "guest friend." Instead, behind his back, Menelaus is a "spy" or "provocateur," the "future enemy." In exchange for hospitality, Priam establishes a "security net"—"a new word," Cassandra observes. "What do words matter? All of a sudden those of us who persisted in saying 'guest friend'—including me—found themselves under suspicion." It isn't long before the king establishes a citywide surveillance network: "Those who had nothing to hide had no reason to fear the king." Nevertheless, the story is the same. The Trojans drag the horse inside the city walls. "Blood flowed through our streets," she recalls, "and the wail Troy uttered dug into my ears; since then I have heard it night and day." One imagines her warning at Mycenae, after this desperation and trauma, muttered with near indifference, and the knowledge of her own death, looming just after Agamemnon's, seen with that same indifference. At least then, she knows, it will be over. There will be no more seeing.

Should one elect to surveil for themselves, "Grave Circle A" is just outside the walls of the citadel. It's here, presumably, where Agamemnon, his wife, Clytemnestra, her lover, Aegisthus, and—why not?—poor Cassandra are rotting in each other's miserable company, down to the last carbon atom. At least if you forget that the *Iliad* is only a poem, *Cassandra* a novel, and the *Oresteia* a cycle of plays. Even those who've never read Homer know the stories, buried deep in our culture, in our language. A Trojan prince absconds with Helen, wife of the Spartan king, and—to defend their honor—the Greeks sail 1,186 ships to the walls of Troy, where for ten years they lay siege. We know what doom is in the large wooden horse, what a poison-tipped arrow means for Achilles's heel. It is said that Helen is the most beautiful woman on earth, the most beautiful to have ever existed (and thus the most treacherous). To accept this beauty and to know a thing or two about men, it's not so farfetched for misogynistic generals and kings to wipe out a civilization and call it her fault. But ten years of siege? Over a thousand ships? All this, as Herodotus wrote, for "the sake of a single Lacedaemonian girl"?

It's certainly poetic to think so.

***

As a writer of fiction, you eventually learn there are itches you have to scratch. It's not as a scholar (ha) or even as an essayist that I approach Cassandra's presence at Troy, her city's destruction, or the ossification of myth into language. I have no formal education in the classics, and certainly can't read or write in Greek or Latin. Instead, I came to this as a novelist—and as someone who loves novels and what novels do.

Years before reading Wolf's *Cassandra*, I'd read and reread David Markson's *Wittgenstein's Mistress*. Markson's narrator, Kate, can't or won't extinguish the events of the Trojan War from her mind, compelled to mention Helen, Paris, Achilles, even Patroclus and "poor Astyanax," in an ongoing, disintegrating cycle of meditations that also includes painters, physicists, writers, composers, and cats. Through Kate, I saw the human side of what had always felt to me like part of the fantasy tableau: fighting, war, glory, strength—all that Xbox stuff. It was Kate, in her loneliness, who first convinced me to search Google Maps for a small Turkish town: "The name of Troy had been changed too, naturally. Hisarlik, being what it was changed to." Indeed, Hisarlik is there, deep in the Çanakkale Province, only a short walk from a small lattice of ruins on a hill labeled "Troia." For me, watching "from the heights of the divine home" (Calasso), Troy stepped out into the light.

Early in the novel, Kate describes the view of the Dardanelles from the walls of Troy: "I even dreamed, for a while, that the Greek ships were beached there still. Well, it would have been a harmless enough thing to dream." Suppose my curiosity in searching for Troy had not been rewarded—suppose there were no ruins at all. Walking on the beach outside Hisarlik, does it matter whether or not Achilles's ashes are beneath the sand? Does it matter, standing at the gates of Mycenae, whether or not there was a Cassandra, a Helen, a Clytemnestra? Or is it more important simply to think so?—a harmless enough thing to dream? If stories are the emotional portals to the past, we should hesitate to discount them. After all, it was only a few years ago that Richard III's crooked spine was hoisted out from beneath a parking lot in Leicester—a king whose most famous words aren't his but Shakespeare's (or the shadow we call Shakespeare).

What's crucial to know is that images like these can exist alongside their realities.

Here are what we consider the realities: Troy was an ancient city located along the waters of the Dardanelles, once known as the Hellespont. A geological layer of broken bones, shards of weapons, and smashed rock indicates a violent battle and mass death circa 1190 B.C. During this time, the citadel at Mycenae was a military stronghold and one of the most important political centers in Greece. Sometime between 1500 and 1100 B.C., there was a great general at Mycenae called Agamemnon. Situated as it is, Troy would have controlled and policed access to the Dardanelles, the only seafaring passage between the Aegean and Black Seas, opening trade access to cities across western Asia. While traveling through Greece and Asia Minor, Wolf posed the question: "Did Homer and the others who handed down the cycle of legends about Troy suspect that in following the myth they were helping to conceal the actual facts? Did they suspect that the Achaean's struggle against the Trojans—whoever they were—was about sea trade routes?" If what Wolf suggests is true, the greatest tale of heroes ever told is a glorification of a war of commerce, an act of violence committed in the name of greed—which sounds far more realistic than a war to reclaim a stolen woman, regardless of how beautiful the real Helen, if there was such a woman, might have been.

***

In *The Marriage of Cadmus and Harmony*, one of Calasso's primary obsessions is the moment at which the unity of mythology shatters into literature. Earlier, I mentioned that it was easy, hovering over the plains of Ilium, to picture Helen *or* Paris making the journey to Mount Ida, depending on which version of the myth we wish to see, at that moment—the way one turns a prism to refract a different sparkle of light. This doubling, Calasso says, is what myth does best: "The repetition of a mythical event, with its play of variations, tells us that something remote is beckoning to us. There is no such thing as the isolated mythical event, just as there is no such thing as the isolated world." But literature surrenders this open-endedness, this ability to permit multiple versions, and with it that remote sense of unity. It tends to operate under the assumption that there is a definitive account, one true version of each story. "The novel, a narrative deprived of variants, attempts to recover them by making the single text to which it is entrusted more dense, more detailed." Literature presents its orphans as immutable. As with Saussure's linguistics, literature isn't necessarily an advance in storytelling—only a dominant technology asserting itself.

In committing language to one version of events, Homer is among the first to wield this technology against the polyphony of mythology. It's with that singular name, Homer, that many poets consolidate their works and become, together, one of the Western world's first authors. This coincides with another transfer of power, from legendary heroes to ordinary people: "The fullness of the Homeric word," Calasso writes, "effortlessly bringing into existence whatever it names, is the last heritage of an earth filled and oppressed by the heroes, by their amorous and cruel trampling." The heroes and their trials are replaced with writing and with literature, while myth ossifies into static language, its metaphors no longer reactive. At the same time, the gods make their final withdrawal from the earth, no longer willing to involve themselves in the lives of humankind. All at once, a mythology of metamorphosing deities, brutal heroes, and shifting stories cements itself into stone and onto papyrus.

All this, of course, because the Greeks lived to sing about it and later write it down. The Trojans did not develop a literature—or an alphabet—of their own. In the real-world ruins of Troy, on the Turkish peninsula, only one artifact provides any hint of the Trojans' writing system: a seal from the early thirteenth century B.C. that, in Luwian hieroglyphs, identifies two scribes by name. In the tradition of Sappho, whose work comes to us only in fragments, or Phrynichus, a playwright with no surviving plays, it seems fitting that the entire linguistic history of this lost civilization comes down to one bronze seal with a man and a woman whose only identity is reduced to their profession: writer.

In the history of writing systems, these hieroglyphs occupy a middle space, composed of both logographic words (as in Chinese) and syllabic cuneiform denoting individual sounds. Like our contemporary memes, Luwian hieroglyphs are "suspended between." The Trojans seem to have been reaching toward an alphabet's creative flexibility, but like so many other languages in earth's history, theirs met with a different kind of technology altogether, its tablets burned and its speakers slaughtered, and from there went no further.

***

That human beings generally don't regard themselves as enmeshed with technology—that we often believe ourselves natural or organic or in some sense biologically pure, a species apart from our creations—is a belief made possible through technologies we've created. This irony (or blasphemy) is at the heart (or core) of Donna Haraway's playful and deeply serious "Cyborg Manifesto": "What might be learned from personal and political 'technological' pollution?"

Writing in 1985, Haraway chose the image of the cyborg as a way to actively subvert the consciousness and thought process brought about by "the terrible historical experience of the contradictory social realities of patriarchy, colonialism, and capitalism." The cyborg, a "monster" of science fiction, aims itself at "the social relations of science and technology, including crucially the systems of myth and meanings structuring our imaginations. The cyborg is a kind of disassembled and reassembled, postmodern collective and personal self." Language is particularly important for Haraway, who saw the plurality of literatures and cultures coalescing into a global commodities market of information: "Communications sciences and modern biologies are constructed by a common move— *the translation of the world into a problem of coding*, a search for a common language in which all resistance to instrumental control disappears and all heterogeneity can be submitted to disassembly, reassembly, investment, and exchange." This is exacerbated, she adds, by "new communications technologies [which] are fundamental to the eradication of 'public life' for everyone," es-

What makes the Borg *Star Trek*'s most terrifying enemy is not their enmeshment with technology. The Federation is equally tangled and reliant. The Borg are terrifying because they assimilate—they absorb, use, and erase difference. Sci-fi aside, the American species of capitalism isn't exactly un-Borg-like. Not only is resistance futile, but all difference, all dissent, is immediately assimilated, and—if not erased—made irrelevant.

pecially "video games and highly miniaturized televisions," which "seem crucial to production of modern forms of 'private life' . . .

High-tech, gendered imaginations are produced here, imaginations that can contemplate destruction of the planet and a sci-fi escape from its consequences."

"Myth," Calasso wrote, "like language, gives all of itself in each of its fragments." In the myth of totalitarian capitalism, we promise our bodies, through technologies we create and market, consequence-free lifestyles and consumption. Via globalized language—especially language of commerce—we promise, as Haraway observes, "ultimate mobility and perfect exchange." Cyborg politics is "the struggle for language and the struggle against perfect communication, against the one code that translates all meaning perfectly." This is a metaphorical or mythical framework for reimagining one's place and one's possibilities within the world. It is, she writes, "to recognize 'oneself' as fully implicated in the world," and "frees us of the need to root politics in identification, vanguard parties, purity, and mothering."

***

The cyborg comes to us via the cinematic imagination, where the truly American myths are made. For those in the United States, as Veronica Esposito writes, "cinema is where we go to see our collective dreams projected skyscraper-high. No other medium has done as much to shape our morals and change the way we live."

In the 1980s, Baudrillard, visiting from France, agreed: "It is not the least of America's charms that even outside the movie theaters the whole country is cinematic. The desert you pass through is like the set of a Western . . . The American city seems to have stepped right out of the movies." If the movies have taught Americans to view their country cinematically, they've simultaneously taught the country how to make itself seen: It aspires toward the story it's been assigned. It wants, cravenly, to perform its myth.

A decade before writing about Cassandra, Solnit published *River of Shadows*, a long, circuitous essay that links the railroad's violent westward expansion with the nascence of motion pictures: "The sight of the railroad out the window had prepared viewers for the kinds of vision that cinema would make ordinary . . . At the same time it made the world itself a theater of sorts, a spectacle." So too did the United States make a spectacle of its own violence and brutality: the "wild Indian" of the West was "tamed" and reintroduced in vaudeville shows and, later, the Hollywood westerns of the twentieth century. It was also, she writes, "the era of rapacious exploitation" as industry stripped the continent of its lumber, minerals, and wildlife: "What was vanishing as ecology was reappearing as imagery."

The West—the land itself—was a draw for many of the earliest American photographers, who made their names with lengthy exposures of this "timeless" or "eternal" landscape. Muybridge, Adams, Weston, and many others documented its beauty as it began to become overly familiar, and ambiguously so, as a warning or a memento. Muybridge especially—at the heart of Solnit's *Shadows*—seems to have loved capturing mountains near calm rivers or lakes, in which their reflected peaks offer two contradictory Wests in one photograph: one crisper, cooler, and climbing up into the heavens; the other already fading as it drops away into darkness.

Taking the western wilderness outside of time, these photographers obscured history with an idealized and lost past. In these images, over a century of landscapes, settlements, and human beings could be shuffled into any order and coexist simultaneously, rightly and wrongly. *This was the West*, the photographs offer, without explanation. In Calasso's terminology, this is a mythic framework; it threatens to subvert the authority of a unified narrative. There is, in these shuffled images, no single story of manifest destiny and exploitation and genocide. They assemble a language, in some sense, and lie in wait for a speaker—even someone who might, like Cassandra, wish to warn us.

"The fundamental metaphor" of American culture, Solnit argues, "is one of travel, movement, progress, exploration, discovery, of going somewhere in search of something new, a metaphor that links Columbus in his boats and Fremont on his trails with the Faradays, the Edisons, the Bells, in their laboratories." If the stillness of the photograph threatened to slow down or freeze American life—if it welcomed contemplation and interpretation—cinema would, to co-opt a phrase of Robert Bresson's, "defeat the false powers of photography." Along with the locomotive, it would not only shift the image back toward real time, but speed that time up—it would accelerate a life, and a country, that could not afford to sit still.

CF. P89

While the early photographs of the West allowed for multiple meanings—a polyphony or plurality of myths asserting themselves—American cinema, entangled in the Hollywood oligopoly, authored and promulgated one narrative, the American Myth. Cinema takes the simultaneous, contradictory images of "lost" peoples, the men who had them killed or driven out because they refused to assimilate, and the landscape on which this invasion took place, and sequences them together as a self-serving story of western expansion and opportunistic, glorious capitalism. "The medium at its most influential," Solnit says, "was to be the fruit of the meeting of huge monopolistic corporations and their fists-ful of dollars with dreamers and self-invented people." By narrating the stories of these venture capitalists and the men they employed to do their killing, decades of Hollywood westerns portrayed to American audiences

> a drama in which they played a heroic role. They embraced the idea that the West was ancient in natural time ... But they wanted it to be utterly new in human history, and thus they tended to ignore or disparage the history of those who had come before them,

the native people and the Spanish settlers. This newness was a vivid part of American identity, the newness of a people who saw themselves just starting out in a landscape of Edenic freshness and infinite resources, infinite possibility. Nineteenth-century Americans liked to contrast this freshness with what they portrayed as the decayed or decadent age of Europe so that lacking a history became a sign of moral virtue rather than cultural poverty. This encouraged the many kinds of erasure of California and western history: the erasure of the Indians, of the personal past, the destruction of resources, species, records. To come west was more often than not to abandon the past.

The movie studios—or the greed they fed from—are largely responsible for America's renewable amnesia, just as literature, in Calasso's CF. P33 account, is responsible for the erasure of Troy. The studios played (and still play) their part in the United States' refusal to take responsibility for its past or see as equal, even human, those from whom it steals its resources. American culture, reflected Baudrillard, is "space, speed, cinema, technology . . . In America cinema is true because it is the whole of space, the whole way of life that are cinematic."

To this day, the Department of Defense exchanges funding and military expertise for final say on a script. In an interview with the DoD's "liaison" to Hollywood, Phil Strub, journalist Amos Barshad asked "if his office ever uses the word *propaganda*. Strub blanched. 'I associate that with something that is not truthful,' he says. 'Something that is put together deliberately to mislead, to brainwash people, to twist the real . . . And maybe you'd accuse me of being too pro-military but to me, the movies we work with, they're morale-improvement.'"

Writing of Ronald Reagan's "illusionist effort to resurrect the American primal scene," Baudrillard saw a generation of voters "neither fired by ambition nor fueled by the energy of repression, but completely refocused upon themselves, in love with business not so much for profit or prestige as for its being a sort of permanence." This was the first generation raised in the movie houses of American cinema's "golden age." In the 1980s, when Reagan threatened that "the real America is back again," banished from collective memory was the complexity and dissensus that characterized the postwar childhoods of his voters, creating in its place a utopian moment of American perfection, reinforced by a lifetime of cinema.

However, Baudrillard adds, "If utopia has already been achieved, then unhappiness does not exist, the poor are no longer credible. If America is resuscitated, then the massacre of the Indians did not happen, Vietnam did not happen . . . The image of America becomes imaginary for Americans themselves." Historic war films and westerns and contemporary desert op films set in Iraq and Afghanistan, in this way, are memorials—they reduce and aestheticize a complex, interconnected history of politics, colonialism, and international power dynamics to form a good and evil, an us versus them. In the eighties—after the counter-narratives of the sixties and seventies threatened to destabilize America's silver-screen image of itself—Reagan, a former actor, elevated "his euphoric, cinematic, extraverted, advertising vision of the artificial paradises of the West to all-American dimensions."

***

River of Shadows is a meditation on the technologies that built the American empire, in myth and reality. But it is, more broadly, about technology itself—neither indictment nor appreciation, but a sort of reverent warning. "Literally," Solnit writes, "a technology is a systemic practice or knowledge of an art." While generally applied to "the scientific and mechanical" realms of human experience—the clang of the engine or the flash of the bulb—"there is no reason not to apply it to other human-made techniques for producing desired results."

A technology, as Solnit redefines it, "is a practice, a technique, or a device for altering the world or the experience of the world." As human beings, we've always surrounded ourselves, enmeshed ourselves, with technology; we have always been Haraway's cyborgs. Metaphor itself is a technology. In fact, by allowing for imaginative production, metaphor may be the ur-technology from which all other technologies spring.

"One of the goals of a book," Guibert writes, "is also to keep a language going, a certain threatened use of language." In *this* book, metaphors react to their halves chemically. Fuel spent, we then dig these metaphors' bones from the dirt. These chemical and archaeological metaphors are units I've chosen to explain and to ornament the importance of language in anti-fascist thought and action. Literature, to which this book aspires, is explanation and ornamentation, description and encryption, braided together in language—crucial and useless.

Metaphor makes possible the individual units of language—itself a technological apparatus that pierces, envelopes, surrounds, and connects us. Prior to the emergence of the Greek alphabet, the mnemonic Homeric epithet—"rosy-fingered dawn, "wine-dark sea," "resourceful Odysseus," "swift-footed Achilles"—helped sustain this oral epic's massive vocabulary. It's easier to memorize and recite over fifteen thousand lines of poetry when half of one line is dedicated to a multidactylic word pairing. Each presents an image for the listener—an image that, after hearing it repeatedly, one's imagination no longer conjures. Helen becomes twinned to her epithets; we no longer see past her clichés.

Presumably, this technique is why the *Iliad* and the *Odyssey*—each a massive work of the imagination, even if they do have roots in history—both appear on papyrus shortly after the emergence of Greek writing itself. After centuries of recitation and memorization, and composed predominantly of images deployed as familiar, ready-made clichés, these stories were the perfect foundational texts for a new

Later, these same written legends would serve as the foundation for theater, whose own original compositions, thousands of years after that, would feed another art form's earliest explorations: the cinema. The imagination often precedes the technological sophistication of its deployment.

way of writing. Where writing itself is concerned, the Greeks borrowed largely from the fully phonetic (sound-based) alphabet of the Phoenicians. In their own alphabet, however, the Greeks were among the first to introduce vowels—the breath that brushes up against the edge of a consonant: the gap of sound between the teeth and the click of the tongue. Vowels—aspirated sound made possible by edges—exist in the poetic imagination of language as breath. "For the ancient Greeks," writes Anne Carson, "breath is consciousness, breath is perception, breath is emotion." Somewhat like the modern *heart* in our song lyrics, for these ancient speakers the chest was "a receptacle of sense impressions . . . Words, thoughts, and understanding are both received and produced by the *phrenes* [translated as *lungs*]. So words are 'winged' in Homer when they issue from the speaker, and 'unwinged' when they are kept in the *phrenes* unspoken." Spoken language is a traveler. It crosses a distance between speaker and listener, and speech itself is set in motion. This shouldn't be a surprise, Carson says: "Such a conception is natural among people in an oral environment . . . Breath is primary insofar as the spoken word is." So too is it only

In her journals, Sontag observes bodily breath as life's visibility: "The 'Art Nouveau' appeal of smoking: manufacture your own pneuma, spirit. 'I'm alive.' 'I'm decorative.'" Here, too, the inseparability of being alive from being seen, of imagining oneself as a thing to be seen.

natural for this breath to manifest itself in writing as vowels, the sounds channeled by the restrictions of the body and sent, winged, on their way.

The Greek alphabet was to have been a limitless, inexhaustible source of phonetic representation—a technology to convey, without literal breath, the breath of language from one to another, regardless of distance. But an actual listener, Carson says, "into whom sounds are being breathed in a continuous stream from the poet's mouth," has a sensual presence that a reader does not:

A reader must disconnect himself from the influx of sense impressions transmitted by nose, ear, tongue and skin if he is to concentrate upon his reading. A written text separates words from one another, separates words from the environment, separates words from the reader (or writer) and separates the reader (or writer) from his environment . . . As separable, controllable units of meaning, each with its own visible boundary, each with its own fixed and independent use, written words project their user into isolation.

Deprived of other senses, a reader is reduced to seeing. What they see—letters, petroglyphs, cuneiform script, abjad, Wingdings—is an ongoing pattern of enclosed images, each representing a sound (as in letters or syllabaries) or an idea (as in glyphs or words). This cleaving of the reader from space and time mirrors the cleaving of their personhood as Aristophanes imagines in Plato's *Symposium*: a whole person of two halves split by a jealous Zeus into two half persons, each seeking to be whole again. It's this edge we look for. It's this frame we want to illuminate, to get a sense of our boundaries. It's these years we count to see the dark chasm of time between moments.

Or, for the lucky ones, to feel it.

III

LITTLE SYMPHONY
FOR THE BODY

At its etymological root, the glyph is something split, something cleaved: a carving. Yet every glyph chipped out of the rock is also an image, a small work of art. Art's oldest root is a fitting together, a joining. As the earliest form of writing, glyphs reveal both the violence and the creativity in language. This tension, this irreconcilability, is a delight. "To catch beauty,"

In *Eros the Bittersweet*, Carson outlines love's relationship with language, and the impossibility of each without a tension that is both temporal and spatial: "In the interval between glance and counterglance, between 'I love you' and 'I love you too,' the absent presence of desire comes alive." There is no desire without absence, without a boundary of flesh or of time: "In letters as in love, to imagine is to address oneself to what is not."

as Carson writes, "would be to understand how that impertinent stability in vertigo is possible." Without this elusiveness, language would not move—nor art, nor knowledge: "To be running breathlessly, but not yet arrived, is itself delightful, a suspended moment of living hope." This tension, where beauty is uncatchable—where so much more is possible because what we want has not yet been rejected—holds open an ancient and special space, and densely dark. To fall under a spell can never be photographed.

Even before he began to die, Guibert observed how his life seemed to be a "foreclosed novel, with all of its characters, its eternal loves . . . its ghosts, and there is no further role to fill, the places are taken, walled up." Years prior, he'd written of his hesitation to indulge his passion for photography: "This attraction frightens me . . . out of one day of one's life one could cut out thousands of instants, thousands of little surfaces, and if one begins why stop?" If one's narrative of resistance goes against the actual life one is living, indeed—when do you stop revising?

In what darkness does one preserve the living self?—or, for lack of a better word, the soul?

Photography, as Barthes writes, has its risks. Seeing has its risks. After he died, Sontag recalled how he "had beautiful eyes, which are always sad eyes." When Sontag died, novelist Sigrid Nunez found the shock of it—"to have been such a person, someone who struck others as too strong and tough, too *alive* to die"— almost an antidote to Sontag's "insistence on her exceptionalism, her refusal to admit that her case was hopeless, that death was not only inevitable, not only near, but *here*."

In *The Ongoing Moment*, Geoff Dyer recalls a conversation he once had with John Berger, who some years before had visited the legendary Henri Cartier-Bresson, then in his eighties. "What struck Berger most about Cartier-Bresson," Dyer remembers, "were his blue eyes which, he said, were 'so tired of seeing.'" When Berger died, Dyer professed that "No one has ever matched [his] ability to help us look at paintings or photographs 'more seeingly,' as Rilke put it in a letter about Cézanne."

When Guibert did begin to die, recording in journal entries and photographs the ongoing deterioration of his young body from AIDS, he observed how "the only things I want to photograph now are at the edge of the night." In one of life's strange echoes, Dyer recalls Diane Arbus's fascination, late in her life, "with what could not be seen in photographs." In one of her final lessons to her students, before she killed herself, she confessed to the pleasures of what is not seen in photographs, what is hidden in the dark—"An actual physical darkness and it's very thrilling for me to see darkness again."

The photographed moments of the past, it is imagined, are entombed. Their story is over. Images of the future are equally severed, stretching out into another narrative we curate and navigate. In this claustrophobic present, it's only natural to claw and scratch at whatever we can to get by, to cope with the panic of an entire world suffocating. It's natural to feel as if one's soul is fading, and it may, in an increasingly surveilled and consumed world, become necessary to again savor transience, to again allow moments to step back into the dark.

Written down, as we've seen, what was once spoken becomes breathless, embalmed in boundaries of ink. Coined from metaphor like the flash of a collapsing star, a new word's light dissipates outward until its darkness and death are writ in the standardized lexicon, until the metaphor is invisible. In these moments, the pursuit is over. Death has arrived. Like a metaphor, an oft-quoted photograph—a photograph that means something—has no future: it is clipped from the ongoing logos of life. What we scratch into the film, onto the paper, into the side of a cliff—these are and have been excisions of greed, stirred by excitement. More than ever, it's with these victims we populate our lives, and through these dead we tell our stories.

Barthes's image of the fastened butterfly resonates personally. Caught in the triangulation of male desire, one is likely, at some point, to hear the word "perfect"—usually leveled at your body or some part of it. This is a difficult complaint in a community that both seems to worship and resent stereotypical standards of male beauty. But "perfect," to me, has never carried the pleasure of a compliment, only the sting of the entomologist's pin. It's a collector's word, and I don't wish to be collected. I don't wish to be made dead.

***

At the Morgan Library in New York, I saw Peter Hujar's portrait of David Wojnarowicz, gaunt and sharply shadowed, dark-eyed, a cigarette in mid drag; and I felt it, around my neck. Love there, and admiration. Grief. Seeing how Hujar saw his lover, friend, and fellow artist seized me entirely. I didn't understand why I was trembling. It just happened as these things happen—and, for me, are happening more and more. In 2018, *T* magazine ran a special issue on the early eighties in New York. On one page, Edmund White remembered friends, writers, and artists who'd died young: "I was just thinking of Allen Barnett, who lived to publish one book of stories . . . He was so angry that he had to die." On another page, the faces of over a hundred artists, choreographers, writers, performers, designers, and cinematographers "lost" to HIV-related illnesses. I sobbed when I saw it. The same thing happened with Tom Bianchi's photographs of Fire Island from the early eighties, in which young men, naked or mostly naked, smile there on the sand with no idea what awaits them. "I could not have imagined," Bianchi writes in *Fire Island Pines*, "that my Polaroids would so suddenly become a record of a lost world—my box of pictures a mausoleum, too painful to visit. When I reopened the box decades later, I found friends and lovers playing and smiling. Alive again." Even this, reread so many times, is hard to transcribe.

I began having sex with men in 2006. HIV is not only a treatable illness but, thanks to PrEP, easier to avoid contracting than ever. I've lost no one to AIDS. I was a child when it decimated queer communities across the world. Because of this, it's taken me a long time to understand that there is still trauma here, that for me to look back and see what has happened, and to see the people— the Reagan administration, state and local governments, charity organizations, and "normal Americans"—who stood by and let it happen, is for me a trauma I'm allowed to feel. It's traumatic to know how many influential figures called it punishment, called it God, and how many millions nodded along with them. It's traumatic that I believed, long after the documented success of antiretroviral therapy, that HIV was certain death. It's traumatic to imagine myself and my friends in that other decade, losing all the men in my life, all while someone laughs on television, where they are paid to say, *You had it coming.*

Yes, they called me faggot, bullied me, threatened me; yes, I pushed myself so deeply into the closet that I thought I was someone else, hurting a lot of people in the process; and yes, I carry scars from those years when I craved physical pain instead of pain I couldn't articulate. But no one I love died, not like that. Not long ago, people like me suffered unimaginably and died in isolation, cut off not only from civil and social apparatuses but often their families; and this happened because those people were like me. Through shunning, violence, intimidation, and legislation, a society had so othered LGBTQ+ individuals that their drawn out and brutal deaths seemed permissible, even desirable. And alongside those deaths, what were a few million drug users, homeless persons, and Black Americans living in abject poverty? Because of white supremacist and heteropatriarchal ideologies, a virus became a weapon of the state, allowed first to proliferate and then, once activists had pushed back hard enough, to be contained, managed, and controlled by federal subsidies and corporate pharmaceutical research.

Not that this "long ago" is necessarily isolated from the present. This "never again," like all others, calls for constant vigilance. In February of 2018, the White House proposed a 20 percent cut in the nation's global HIV/AIDS fund, which would lead, according to a report issued by ONE.org, to "nearly 300,000 deaths and more than 1.75 million new infections each year." On June 1 of 2019, the president announced that the United States would "celebrate LGBT Pride Month and recognize the outstanding contributions LGBT people have made to our great Nation," despite everything his administration and party have done to strip

Nor does "never again" mean that one should only watch out for the government's deployment of a virus against highly specific communities, as the Trump administration's overwhelming, widespread, and malicious negligence w/r/t COVID-19 has made clear.

trans persons of their safety and their rights, and to obstruct federal and state protections for queer families and workers. It's especially tempting to ask this transphobic autocrat what he believes the T stands for when he reminds the nation to celebrate LGBT people, but that's beside the point. It's not ignorance that emanates from the White House. It is not a politics in conflict. No matter how many rainbow emoji Trump tweets, his queer politics is death, hate, and exclusion. It is a legacy of abuse, and perhaps it's only natural to feel it across generations, to break down sobbing when I discover another artist or writer or human being who was, not that many years ago, "so angry that he had to die."

For Wojnarowicz himself, the 2010s were something of a renaissance. In a retrospective at the Whitney Museum, *History Keeps Me Awake at Night*, we are reminded that Wojnarowicz "came to prominence in New York in the 1980s, a period marked by creative energy, financial precariousness, and profound cultural changes." We are to recognize that time period in our own and, with it, Wojnarowicz's anger.

In truth, *renaissance* is a cruel word to give to someone who died at thirty-seven. But we do love him. We do, these days, need him, trapped as we are in a moment of political terror. And what else? We are dangerously close to cynicism, but angry enough to have hope. We are no longer interested in compromise. Men, we agree, have had their chance. White women can no longer be trusted to uphold feminism, not while they cling to white supremacy. We are anti-racist and anti-fascist and prison abolitionists; we rejoiced when Bill Cosby received his sentence. We canceled Woody Allen, Kevin Spacey, Harvey Weinstein, and Al Franken with equal fervor. We are uninterested in what they think. We could really use a kind of miracle or martyr, or at the very least a leader.

It seems inevitable that, in a time of such divisiveness, *we* would become a disingenuous pronoun that both paid and un-

paid pundits brandish without consent. I'm often guilty, too: my
points are more convincing if I ventriloquize your voice alongside CF. P6
mine. Are we really doing this? Is this what we want? When did
we decide this was okay? As usual, Adorno said it best: "To say
'we' and mean 'I' is one of the most recondite insults." More often
than not, *we* is an erasure, a linguistic illusion that you or I have
endorsed some third person's opinion, politics, or decisions. Deployed in politicized spaces, the subtext of we—i.e., *I* didn't need
to ask *you*—is a violation of political agency.

What's dangerous in maligning *we*, however, is how badly I—a
cisgender white man living in America—need to hear these voices.
Often, the contemporary we is a backlash against centuries of a
white cishet male monolith, which includes the we in the Constitu-
tion. It's a backlash voiced by women, Black and Indigenous Americans, people of color, trans and nonbinary persons, and persons
with disabilities. As Wesley Morris writes for *The New York Times*,
"Groups who have been previously marginalized can now see that
they don't have to remain marginalized. Spending time with work
that insults or alienates them
has never felt acceptable. Now
they can do something about
it." Morris casts this moment
as an inversion of the "culture
wars" (so branded, but closer to
cultural terrorism) of the eighties and nineties, when artists like
Wojnarowicz faced censorship and humiliation from the religious
right. After pushing their work to extremes and waging costly legal
and political campaigns—including, in Wojnarowicz's case, the
very right to survive—the oppressed are now closer to power than
ever. "This territory," Morris writes, "was so hard won that it must
be defended at all times, at any costs. Wrongs have to be righted.
They can't affect social policy—not directly. They can, however,

> I can't speak for him, but having spent time
> with Wojnarowicz's work, I get the impression
> that "we" is a power he'd have deeply distrusted.
> It's something the marginalized, politically
> manipulated, and rhetorically violated would
> naturally distrust.

LITTLE SYMPHONY FOR THE BODY   151

amend the culture." It's in this sense that we is linguistic action. We cosign or cancel speech, endorse or excoriate art, all the while presuming that any *I* can borrow any *you*. To say "we" amplifies our voices as one, an assumption of power.

In most contemporary rhetoric, we is the leftist (or leftish) counterpart to the right's fantasy of the "silent majority" (as if any of them could ever shut the fuck up). In Canetti's terminology, it might function as a kind of "crowd crystal"—structures that "can be comprehended and taken in at a glance. Their unity is more important than their size." It's important that we see the crowd through this crystal and associate its power, its authority, accordingly—even if unearned or undeserved. As it concerns early twenty-first-century life, particularly in the United States, the pronoun is often visual shorthand for José Ortega y Gasset's "masses": "those who demand nothing special of themselves, but for whom to live is to be every moment what they already are . . . mere buoys that float on the waves." The culture of the masses, as Ortega y Gasset wrote from Spain on the eve of civil war, "crushes beneath it everything that is different, everything that is excellent, individual, qualified and select. Anybody who is not like everybody, who does not think like everybody, runs the risk of being eliminated."

While Morris's essay is sensitive and observant, and while I'm grateful to have read and reread it, my first impulse upon seeing its subheading ("Should art be a battleground for social justice?") was to throw it across the room and tweet something like, "Do we really need another man whispering 'art for art's sake' as he pins us against the wall?" This is what our experience of public life has done to me as a "marginalized" artist. I carry so much anger that even the threat of some man saying *Let's not get carried away* triggers rage. Or perhaps more exact: revenge. I want to crush beneath *our* imagined moral homogeny what is different in Morris's ideas—or any ideas I find immediately, triggeringly challenging, however excellent, individual, qualified, or select.

In the same way, I want to believe we need Wojnarowicz's art. I want to prescribe it for *us*. But in truth I can only say that I need it: his juxtapositions, the shadows in his photographs, the narrative ambition of his paintings—exuberant perversions of renaissance epics. *Close to the Knives*, his "memoir of disintegration," is a revelation in all ancient senses. Like many queers in the seventies, Wojnarowicz grew up neglected and abused, selling sex by the time he was fifteen so he could afford to eat. As an artist, he received no formal training—only critique from other artists, including Peter Hujar, whose ravaged body became one of Wojnarowicz's most enduring subjects. Hujar's face and hands and feet, photographed on his deathbed in 1987, found their way into a collage, lacquered over with a fiery indictment of the society that let this happen to a man he loved; and then Wojnarowicz, too, died, and with so much art left unmade.

Reading Wojnarowicz today—that is, as he once put it, "in a country where an actor becomes the only acceptable president . . . a man whose vocation is to persuade with words and actions an audience who wants to believe whatever he tells them"—is invigorating. Art "can be reparatory," Morris writes, "a means for the oppressed and ignored to speak," and Wojnarowicz's anger makes us feel, makes me feel, as if it's my right to demand silence from those I perceive to have oppressed queer people, or even those who just don't have the luck of being queer. I feel as if it's my right to shun artworks in which I don't recognize myself or my friends. To not see oneself mirrored in culture feels like abuse, every renewed act of erasure newly unbearable.

While Morris writes about art specifically, his essay reflects an overall tendency in this shattered culture toward separating, totally, that which we call bearable from that which we decide is not. This is the subject of Sarah Schulman's *Conflict Is Not Abuse: Overstating Harm, Community Responsibility, and the Duty of Repair.* "At many levels of human interaction," she points out, "there is an opportunity to conflate discomfort with threat, to mistake internal anxiety for exterior danger, and in turn to escalate rather than resolve." As social creatures, communication and negotiation are human responsibilities. Activities that work against communication—shunning, silencing, and enlisting the power of the state to punish rather than resolve—shirk this responsibility, and are unfortunately common among vulnerable persons, for whom withdrawal and refusal are often the only communication skills they possess. This leaves both parties trapped—one behind a locked door they won't open, the other outside. Schulman describes her struggle to understand her colleagues, who, despite their progressive politics, have developed an "almost prescribed instinct to punish, using the language originated initially by a radical movement but now co-opted to deny complexity, due process, and the kind of in-person, interactive conversation that produces resolution." This language is that of "abuse," which has a perpetrator and a victim.

In situations of abuse (ask yourself: is this a power struggle or does this person have power over me?), victims are indeed blameless. But Schulman's thesis outlines how what often feels like abuse is instead conflict—a point of pain in need of resolution, arrived at only through honest and open communication, which can, and often does, hurt: "the collapse of Conflict and Abuse is partly the result of a punitive standard in which people are made desperate, yet ineligible, for compassion." The state and its systems of power withhold assistance and compassion from those who are not "eligible." This creates a system where the identity of victim is desired, if only to ensure one is met with compassion instead of derision. "This concept," Schulman writes, "is predicated on a need to enforce that one party is entirely righteous and without mistake, while the other is the Specter, the residual holder of all evil." Anyone who endured the punditry after the 2016 elections will understand why labeling oneself an economic or demographic victim can be toxic. In a sociological refusal to communicate, sixty-three million voters escalated decades of capitalist-driven conflict by turning their pain into a sacrosanct identity, regardless of how it would, and has, hurt millions of people far more severely than any pain, however legitimate, those voters felt.

As part of the totalizing mythography of personalities capitalism imposes upon living human beings, the outsized perception of abuse where there is only conflict is drawing a new kind of map, a new axis of personae. As more and more have or perceive real or simulated access to the civic and socioeconomic punishment apparatuses that govern who is and who is not us, our culture—from its politicians to its artists all the way down to its least valued of consumers—is charting a *victimography*: a system of social navigation where conflicts are permanent, where identities are fixed, and where agency is neutralized like never before.

***

Schulman's ideas on conflict, communication, escalation, abuse, and repair encourage an individual acceptance of responsibility, however small, for as many of the conflicts in one's life as possible. Yet it remains necessary to distinguish these conflicts from abuse. What's interesting about Schulman's essay is how it intersects with urgent questions of speech, de-platforming, and cancelation. Her insistence upon open and respectful communication seems like an inversion of the tactics of silence, shunning, exclusion, and sometimes of violence used by anti-fascist groups for decades to combat authoritarian politics. The strategies of anti-fascism seem to contradict everything Schulman says in her plea toward mutual understanding and conflict resolution, but only in the way that shouting over Ann Coulter, for example, seems like an infringement upon her right to incite violence through free speech.

The error here is to call fascism a conflict.

A primary goal of Mark Bray's *Antifa: The Anti-Fascist Handbook* is to illuminate the "trans-historical terror of fascism," which is never a "defeated" enemy but a constant reactionary threat as long as inequality and suffering are tolerated. History is not fixed or written but being written. That post-Holocaust slogan—"Never again!"—is not a fact, observation, or conclusion, but a plea for understanding. As Bray writes, "History is a complex tapestry stitched together by threads of continuity and discontinuity . . . [Anti-fascism] is an argument about the historical continuity between different eras of far-right violence and the many forms of collective self-defense that it has necessitated across the globe over the past century." As evidenced by what's happened in recent years in the United States, Brazil, India, and several countries in Europe, it could indeed happen again; and one needs to recognize it, contain it, and drive it back out of sight. These tactics don't seek to understand the conflict and work toward resolution because there is no understanding, nor resolution; there is, in fact, no conflict. Fascism is abuse, and its evangelists know it. As Bray says, "The point here is not tactics; it is politics." Just as an abusive parent or partner has no right to demand that his victim sit down and hear his case (again: "power over," not "power struggle"), a political system that is predicated on the oppression and elimination of human beings from the populace based on race, legal history, nationality, gender, sexual orientation, citizenship, or ability has no right to a national platform, and merits resistance over resolution. Fascism assumes a false mask of victimhood—one that seems like a politics in conflict—in order to undermine those who'd speak against it. But fascism is not a politics in conflict: it is a politics of abuse on a national and transnational scale. Anti-fascism seeks a way out of trauma; fascism governs with it.

**

Those sixty-three million votes: was each an act of abuse? I *want* to say yes. As Bray indicates, "It is clear that ardent Trump supporters voted for their candidate either *because of* or *despite* his misogyny, racism, ableism, Islamophobia, and many more hateful traits." For me and millions of others, these votes felt cruel, and while I'm no longer sure about calling each one abusive, I don't question my choice to end every relationship I had with anyone who used that vote to inflict such irresponsible, widespread harm.

Supremacist ideologies don't need that many fervent supporters; what they do need is indifference (including, in the case of the United States, an overwhelming nonvoting population). In the case of Trump voters, Bray writes, "it is always important to distinguish between ideologues and their capricious followers, yet we cannot overlook how these popular bases of support create the foundations for fascism to manifest itself."

Every fascist regime has snuck into power through legal means with a relatively small majority. In 1930, the Nazis received 18.3 percent of the vote. When Vittorio Emanuele III appointed Mussolini as prime minister in 1922, the PNF only held thirty-five of more than 500 seats. In 2016, Trump received over 2.8 million fewer votes than Clinton. As I write this, there are 31 states—plus D.C.— with party registration. In those states, registered Democrats outnumber Republicans by 12 million; yet Republicans control 61 of the 99 state legislative bodies and hold a majority in the Senate.

It's hard to see class in America—to see poverty, for example, as an identity—because the American fabrication is that today's poor, through obedience and hard work, will be rich tomorrow. It's a story that hides, in plain sight, an oppressed class that serves as a ready-made voting base for the rich, as long as the rich grant them whiteness, heteronormativity, male supremacy, or some other power over those more deeply oppressed. They may not champion the oppression of others, but they do go along with it—or turn from the horror of it—as a price paid for a seat at the table.

It's difficult to accept responsibility for this transaction, so enticing is its reward: state-sponsored victimhood. To take an example from Schulman, the white queer community doesn't want to hear that today, "with gay marriage and parenthood prevalent, and the advent of gay nuclear families and normalized queer childbirth . . . white queer families realign with the state that held them in pervasive illegality less than a generation ago." At the same time, this community still often sees itself as unable to do harm, so entrenched is its history with victimhood. To challenge this is perceived as antiqueer: of course we have the right to families, to suburbs, to lattes and plaid. But so, too, do white gays and lesbians, in their newfound positions of power, have newfound responsibility to uphold the greater community, and to use their privilege to resolve conflicts between the state and the trans community, between their neighbors and queers of color, not to mention other oppressed and persecuted communities, queer or not.

There is a similarity in refusal, Schulman says, in the supremacist and the victim: "For the Supremacist, this refusal comes from a sense of entitlement; that they have an inherent 'right' not to question themselves. Conversely, the unrecovered traumatized person's refusal is rooted in a panic that their fragile self cannot bear interrogation." For the conflicted, seeing their pain mirrored in another can become a way to justify pain: *at least she feels what I feel*, or even *at least he's worse off than me*. What this creates is an ongoing and mutually reflective theater of trauma in which everyone is a victim, exempt from responsibility, beyond repair.

***

Like martyrs and monsters, the victim is a place, a container. Unlike martyrs and monsters, we know precisely how to get there. It takes unique and enormous efforts to arrive at martyrdom or monsterhood; yet, for most people, it's easier than not to become a victim—though it's generally a one-way trip. To leave would be to renounce one's citizenship of victimhood, or Schulman's "eligibility for compassion."

All of these are, by design, dehumanizations. To confine anyone, in any sense, is an effort to dehumanize, but especially with regard to identity and agency. This is why, as Foucault suggested in the 1970s, even the criminal justice system has spent centuries morphing from a public display of violent punishment into a curio of isolated, neutralized victims—a criminological victimography. "The question is no longer simply: 'Has the act been established and is it punishable?' . . . A whole set of assessing, diagnostic, prognostic, normative judgements concerning the criminal have become lodged in the framework of penal judgement." Foucault refers here to the expertise sought during our highly stylized, ritualistic trials—psychologists, forensic analysts, medical professionals, historians, all of whom are urged, directly and indirectly, to produce truths about the criminal or the act committed, and all of whom are, with respect to their expertise, themselves isolated and divided in their labors.

"The criminal's soul," Foucault adds, "is not referred to in the trial merely to explain his crime and as a factor in the juridical apportioning of responsibility . . . it is because it too, as well as the crime itself, is to be judged and to share in the punishment." Under monarchies, where a crime was an offense against the king, it was in the king's interest to torture, dismember, brand, and otherwise spectacularly scar or destroy the criminal in a public capacity; his soul, in a sense, was eliminated. But under democracy, "Why would society eliminate a life and a body that it could appropriate?" Instead of becoming the king's property, the democratically punished man "will be rather the property of society, the object of a collective and useful appropriation." Through prosecutorial discipline, the criminal is made a victim of his crime; so guilty, he can no longer be trusted with his soul. "Through imprisonment, one has security for someone, one does not punish him . . . The duration of the penalty has meaning only in relation to possible correction, and to an economic use of the corrected criminal." It's for this reason that the poor are sentenced so much more severely—as are the Black, Indigenous, queer, brown, and so on. Or simply the vocal left, as the increasingly appalling penalties leveled against protestors have revealed. "Discipline," Foucault concludes, "is the unitary technique by which the body is reduced as a 'political' force at the least cost and maximized as a useful force."

Another project of Foucault's *Discipline & Punish* is to trace the juridical concern with assault, murder, and violence done to the person, to an obsession with "offences against property." This was accelerated with the overt creation of "lower strata" and their "conditions of existence," the illegality of which "was a perpetual factor in the increase of crime." Whereas the destitute were once a charitable concern, the shift of illegality from person to property helped malign the poor as a "criminal class."

The obsession with visibility in criminal punishment is why Bentham's Panopticon remains the ideally organized prison—and why, too, that prison has spilled over, in spirit, into the daily life of nearly everyone on the planet. The genius of the Panopticon, Foucault says, is "to induce in the inmate a state of conscious and permanent visibility that assures the automatic functioning of power . . . surveillance is permanent in its effects, even if it is discontinuous in its action." A key feature of the victimized criminal—and the victimized person overall—is a total depletion of privacy. Victims require surveillance. To prove innocence—to prove that you didn't deserve what has happened to you, where you're at in life, what you have to show

Again, criminal "justice" leaves its economic mark: privacy is now a luxury in capitalist nations, and the poor are deprived of it in almost every capacity.

for yourself; or to prove the inevitability, the circumstances, of your actions—those capable of passing judgment upon you must have access to myriad sources of knowledge to produce their truth: they must know, we must know, everything about you.

As Canetti points out, one of the rare opportunities to escape one's visibility—one's being seen as a victim—is to vanish into a crowd of others: "One of the most striking traits of the inner life of a crowd is the feeling of being persecuted, a peculiar angry sensitiveness and irritability directed against those it has once and forever nominated as enemies." The crowd offers a relief from the burdens and fears of being isolated, literally or visually. It lends political strength to an individual long deprived of it—whether legally, as with persons who've committed felonies and others liquidated of their citizenship, or economically.

This, of course, is why autocrats work so hard to convince their crowds that they've been wronged, that someone has stolen from them or assaulted them or otherwise sinned against them. It is in his interest that they feel traumatized. "Anyone who wants to rule men first tries to humiliate them," Canetti writes, "to trick them out of their rights and their capacity for resistance, until they are as powerless before him as animals . . . His ultimate aim is to incorporate them into himself and to suck the substance out of them." Canetti's metaphors are of eating, of domestication and consumption. The victim is "seen as meat whilst it is still alive, and so intensely and irrevocably seen as meat that nothing can deflect the watcher's determination to get hold of it." He evokes the trapping of animals through the power of transformation, through disguise—the wolf, as it were, in sheep's clothing—which "may be termed flattery. The animal is told 'I am like you. I am you. You can safely let me come near you.'" To remain controllable, the animal, the victim, must remain visible; it must not be allowed to change, to disguise itself, to hide, to grow, to heal. While it may come with a little prize of its own—protection, excitement, even just a cheap thrill—to belong to a victimography is to lose agency over one's own life, almost always for the benefit of some nearby, watchful predator; it is to be rebranded and sold as a commodity for someone else's profit. Which confronts us all with interesting, important questions. What use am I, for example, and who is profiting from my trauma? How has my pain, and pains adjacent, been weaponized and turned against others to stoke greater conflict?

Conflict is profitable. Not only is this obvious in two hundred years of U.S. foreign policy, but in millennia of art and entertainment: escalation is dramatic, and drama, if it doesn't affect us directly, is cathartic. There's a reason journalists crank the apocalypse up to eleven every time the president tweets. It keeps readers coming back. Resolution, however, is unprofitable. A played-out resolution is not a drama but an education. Resisting this is not easy, fast, or efficient—three "values" Americans cherish. To be conflicted, to explore one's accountability in a relationship—this is not what makes an individual spectacularly eligible for compassion. Only victimhood opens that coffer, and whoever screams loudest gets the prize.

What is needed is a queering of compassion. To move beyond the truly rare (but extant) binaries of perpetrator and victim, it's important that every individual recognize their existence in a continuum of conflict, and seek to resolve and repair rather than escalate and destroy. We—and here I do mean we—must question individual guilt, which is rooted in action, rather than shame, which is entrenched in identity. Because when we insist upon the binary—that everyone is either perpetrator or victim—the cost is literal human life.

To see this, one need only look to all the Black Americans murdered by police, summoned by a white neighbor's perceived victimhood, amplified by the aesthetics of entertainment.

Is it so revolutionary to say that every human being is eligible for compassion? That persons of any gender or sexuality, any skin color, any ability, any legal or migratory status, any age, receive the same compassionate understanding as any other, responsible only for their actions and not the identities coerced upon them by others? The we I want to belong to is the we that recognizes our vast diversity of pain—the we that understands we've been assigned this pain for someone else's profit, and that we need no longer give them want they want. To reserve compassion only for victims deemed eligible is to accept an arbitrary division, one in which the state can deem some of us worthy of aid and exclude others, meanwhile ensuring that the victims never speak to one another, competing as they must to remain in their places, and the "perpetrators"—the property of the state—never speak at all.

These cartographical metaphors—a mythography, a victimography—come easily to a culture in which the human experience of space has come to outweigh (or outvalue) so significantly the experience of time. To imagine identities fixed on a map is to call attention to Western culture's obsession with space—which, unlike time, can be seen, or at least imagined in visual registers. Even a clock doesn't show time as an accumulation—only as a coordinate, only where one is at in time.

To be socially human is to be neither exclusively spatial nor temporal but both, equally and always—beings-in-time. If this seems unrecognizable or unintuitive it's because our culture has been deeply, disturbingly warped by an overwhelmingly spatial sensibility—the image, the commodity, the boundaries of our plots or properties, of our cells. As Walter Benjamin wrote from Weimar Berlin, photography "freed the hand of the most important artistic functions which henceforth devolved only upon the eye looking into a lens. Since the eye perceives more swiftly

The hand, as Canetti writes, is inextricable from language: "As a man watched his hands at work, the changing shapes they fashioned must gradually have impressed themselves on his mind. Without this we should probably never have learnt to form symbols for things, nor, therefore, to *speak*." It is human hands that made shadows—that told stories—upon cavern walls. It is hands, as Canetti writes, that spark the transformative imagination: "The hand which scoops up water is the first vessel. The fingers of both hands intertwined are the first basket."

than the hand can draw, the process of pictorial reproduction was accelerated so enormously that it could keep pace with speech." However, because these works of art were no longer discrete objects, they lost their individual "presence in time and space," their "unique existence at the place where it happens to be." This uniqueness Benjamin calls the "aura," and the aura is precisely "that which withers in the age of mechanical reproduction." This is exacerbated by "the desire of contemporary masses to bring things 'closer' spatially and humanly . . . Every day the urge grows stronger to get hold of an object at very close range by way of its likeness, its reproduction." Ultimately, this changes the way art is made: "To an ever greater degree the work of art reproduced becomes the work of art designed for reproducibility." This pushes art away from its mystery, its ritual or spiritual nature of creating an aura. "The instant the criterion of authenticity ceases to be applicable to artistic production," as is the case with photographic negatives, "the total function of art is reversed. Instead of being based on ritual, it begins to be based on another practice—politics." Transformed into a reproducible commodity, art's economic fetishization has political and, ultimately, spiritual consequences.

None of this is a surprise in a culture as capitalistically totalitarian as ours. It is capitalism, after all, that divides our labor so systematically, so categorically, as Lukács writes, that "it reduces space and time to a common denominator and degrades time to the dimension of space." This, too, is why we tend to imagine ourselves, our lives, our days as containers—how much can we have? how much can we be? how much can we learn? how much can we collect? These translations of time into volume affect the corporate vocabulary we tend to employ in organizing—in scheduling—our lives. Are we productive? Are we managing ourselves? Are we main- CF. P90 taining our capital—intellectual, social, and emotional—with procedures of "self-care?" Are we making the most (i.e., maximizing efficiency) of our lives? You only live once: In the spatially imagined life, how much life can you fit?

***

With corporatized language, even the most temporal aspects of life or of art can be reimagined as space. In my own life, I started noticing this phenomenon when I began to add "listen to music" to my to-do list. Simply putting on an album and enjoying it—something that used to seem so natural, so automatic—had become difficult. I missed listening. At some point, I'd become a customer—or, in the vocabulary of technology companies, a user.

In one room, I have a turntable and sixty or seventy vinyl records. In other rooms, I have speakers connected to wireless receivers. What this means is that I can listen to my records in only one room, but I can listen, conveniently, to one of 16,656 files in any room. The files themselves I select and sequence primarily to match an activity—reading, cooking, drinking—and only secondarily on what the artist has made. This is music as décor.

Like most tech platforms, iTunes is marketed as access but is in practice a bureaucratic briar patch that often leaves me with a song I've settled for, not sought. Which is how these platforms are supposed to work: they manage what content their sponsors prefer you to see, hear, or read. Netflix, too, hasn't given its users what they want so much as shaped how they engage its content, allowing a significantly reduced catalogue (but only after wiping out its competition).

Apple, Inc., has always been transparent about this. In the late nineties, Steve Jobs told *Businessweek* that "people don't know what they want until you show it to them." In every speech Jobs ever gave, you hear the echo of the drug dealer, promising amazement in exchange for cash, for becoming hooked on something new. His legacy infects every platform people in capitalized nations use on a daily basis: each algorithm serves its dealer, not its user. All we have to do is give away as much labor as we can to refine these networks of advertising and surveillance. To do otherwise would be to inconvenience—even isolate—ourselves.

It's in listening that I remind myself of the passion in sharing time with music, which has nothing to do with the way I've been trained by tech companies to use it. This is why I keep the records. This is why, in being alone with analog music, I remember a freedom iTunes has always lied about: I remember what it's like to feel.

I want to be careful. I'm not saying younger generations don't know how to listen to music, nor that physical media are somehow more real. But something has happened to our relationship with music, and we are emotionally impoverished because of it. It's easy to misattribute this shift, as Bono did in an interview with *Rolling Stone*: "Music has gotten very girly." You may recall one of the band's more recent albums if only for its sudden appearance in your iTunes library as a "gift" from Apple. If you listened to it, you heard the gap between the band Bono seems to think he's a part of and the audial décor they are. But what does he mean by "girly"?:

Admittedly, it's difficult to write this outside of nostalgia's haze. The vinyls are proxies for the CDs I grew up with, purchased from incense-smogged stores in strip malls and big-box chain retailers. Their booklets I'd flip through as I lay in bed. This is how I learned to be angry, how to think, to amplify and articulate my moods, to speak against, and ultimately to write. Music is the teenager's doorway to poetry; and for me poetry opened door upon door. I did this by listening.

> Hip-hop is the only place for young male anger at the moment—
> and that's not good. When I was 16, I had a lot of anger in me.
> You need to find a place for it and for guitars . . . The moment
> something becomes preserved, it is fucking over. You might as
> well put it in formaldehyde. In the end, what is rock & roll?
> Rage is at the heart of it.

Beyond Bono's gendering of emotions, he does have a point. When it comes to mainstream music, hip-hop is the sole locus not only of anger but of despair, powerlessness, isolation, protest, frustration, lust, and dynamic joy. Hip-hop is where mainstream music allows feelings. Nearly everything else—from Katy Perry to whatever Bon Iver is supposed to be—is cleansed of difficult emotion, of hard-to-hold feelings. There are exceptions—individual, highly successful artists who give far more than what little we expect from them. But overall, hip-hop is the only genre of mainstream music that hasn't been gentrified.

Gentrified music is music that sidesteps the artful expression of rage, depression, loneliness, and suffering. These are difficult feelings, and to empathize with them would be to recognize our own sidestepped sufferings. Music purged of these feelings is accessible, marketable—not necessarily for the musicians but for the corporations distributing their music, including Apple. With iTunes, music is more tediously classified, tagged, and commodified than ever, complete with playlists catered for eerily specific activities, such as "pure yoga," "study beats," or "get up and go." This algorithmic approach to music maximizes profit, and so does its inherent downplay of music's seriousness as art. If a protest song, say, is divested of its cultural significance, it's just entertainment, a way to fill space. It deflects away from the power structures it criticizes, as those structures benefit from music's commodification and distribution. Rage becomes "noise." Sorrow and grief become "depressing." Emotional complexity becomes impolite, vanishing not only from our public spaces—restaurants, shopping centers, the radio—but even our private ones. Why feel when you could motivate yourself, when you could get up and go? Why spend so much time being sad, being angry?

It's no shock that hip-hop resists gentrification. "Like few other musical forms before it," Kevin Young writes in *The Grey Album*, "hip-hop is almost painfully aware of its own history. More like baseball, or boxing, hip-hop believes that its history, filled with struggle, early triumph, and exploitation, is also the history of America; and as in the national pastime or the sweet science, hip-hop insists that any view of history must include race in the mix."

To gentrify hip-hop would be to eliminate it, tethered as it is not only to Black culture but to Black culture's critique on America's ongoing segregation, oppression, and extermination of its Black citizens. Even white rappers, permanently conspicuous, can't gentrify hip-hop. Nor can particularly wealthy musicians—such as Jay Z, whose ownership of a streaming service contributes to the way music is used rather than listened to—dismantle the aesthetic of resistance innate in hip-hop. If anything, hip-hop has aggressively worked to un-gentrify cities, or at least delay gentrification. Today, it is hip-hop, more than any other genre, that demands rage against suffering and racism, against policy that favors wealth over human beings. It is hip-hop that amplifies grief as our government continues to abandon the poor to drugs, disease, starvation, and violence, not to mention as it continues to murder Black men, women, and non-binary persons with impunity.

An appreciation of hip-hop is Young's last "chorus" in *The Grey Album*, a unique exhumation of how Black culture shaped and still shapes American life as we know it, right down to language: "The black vernacular is not a site of marginalization but of imagination and even infiltration, helping invent the music and meaning of the language we might best call *American* . . . It is black culture that is the dominant culture. English broken here." Young's book convinces us, without any doubt, that "American culture is black culture."

As opposed to the "harmony" of music-as-décor, hip-hop makes as much noise as possible: "Too often black folks are the noise in the culture seen as sonorous without us. If only they'd keep it down!" Tracing AAVE, Young observes that Black Americans are "not immigrants but *imports* to this experiment . . . in our very outsiderness to the language, we forged a sense of belonging." Rather than try to blend in, to homogenize with the part of America that believes itself to be "white," Black culture sets itself apart. Proclaiming difference—loudly—is the basis for resisting gentrification; it is the line that cannot be blurred, crossed, or erased. It's the graffiti that keeps those afraid to feel on the other side of the freeway, in emotional exile.

This is important because music has a unique role in the United States. It's our art of tough times. It's music that speaks of the allures and anxieties of the sixties, and it's music that separates Reagan's white eighties of dance and drug-fueled, glitzy rock from its contemporaneous hip-hop critiquing state-sponsored terrorism against Black communities.

Now, entering the third decade of this new century of crumbling civil rights, a resurgence of fascism has reawakened a politics of protest in mainstream music. In January of 2017, *The New York Times* interviewed the duo Run the Jewels, who thread "social commentary and politics into their giddy homages to psilocybin and marijuana." Coming away with a playlist of protest songs "given the current wave of discontent on *both sides* of American politics" (emphasis mine, since journalists continue to frame the former president's Nazi base as misunderstood), the *Times* piece reflects on music as a medium not only of political consciousness but of things that aren't easy to hear.

Conversely, music that looks away from politics and pain is rightfully suspicious. Writing of Killer Mike's 2012 track "Reagan," El-P tells the *Times* that "everyone has to choose a side. An ethos. You stand up for what you think is right . . . You don't stand there and you don't watch violations of humanity go uncontested." Of another song—Prince's "Sign of the Times"—he recalls how "it was the first time I had really heard him say anything this directly. It opened me up a little bit, turn my brain a little bit more . . . He'd already taken me this far. When the moment came for him to say, 'Now I need you to listen,' I was right there." This sudden shift seems a tradition in Black art, from Beyoncé's "Formation" to Billie Holiday's "Strange Fruit," in which an artist who seems apolitical (read: comfortable for white people) is suddenly political, even confrontational.

In *Blues Legacies and Black Feminism*, Angela Y. Davis identifies this split: "As long as Holiday's work appeared to be without manifest social content, she was praised lavishly by critics . . . Since 'Strange Fruit' was designed unambiguously to prick the conscience of those who were content to remain oblivious to racism, it was inevitable that many critics would dismiss it as propaganda." But because Holiday came to music at a "moment characterized by an accelerated process of individualization in the black community," the listening public was able to identify Holiday's *personal* pain within the song, her voice itself bearing witness to lynching in a nation that didn't see her as a person. She could not have done this, Davis argues, without first establishing herself as "a jazz musician who worked primarily with the idiom of white popular song." These cliché laments of love and loneliness, rendered in her haunting voice, gave her white America's ear. Once she had it, she sang what they didn't want to hear.

***

Commodity fetishism has been at the heart of the music industry in America since its conception. Listeners have always been, in part, users: selecting the mood for a dinner party, or shying away from explicit lyrics for gatherings with people you don't know well. But what Apple, Spotify, and other corporations have done is simplify our usage of music, marketing its use primarily for mood or activity rather than artistic quality or critical acclaim. (Spend fifteen minutes with a group of gay men armed with a Bluetooth speaker and you'll see what I mean.)

The most significant change is that it's easier than ever to pay money to use what you do not own. One need not purchase a single album, or even know anything about jazz, to transform an apartment into a "piano bar" or "jazz club"—to decorate with "chill jazz." This lack of ownership is troubling: our playlists and libraries of music now resemble "our" tweets or Facebook posts—that is, not ours at all but a corporation's, leased to us for creation, curation, and usage. There are people, of course, who still purchase albums digitally and physically, but for the first time in history the majority of listeners are streaming music they do not own. According to Nielsen, streaming services (*not* including internet radio) now account for 54 percent of all audio consumption. To call this gentrification shouldn't surprise anyone who's been gentrified out of owning a home, consigned instead to renting someone else's property; nor should it shock a nation now gentrified out of healthcare, renting our health from insurance companies.

Again, I'm reminded of Wojnarowicz, dying of a disease his government refused to acknowledge, doing time "in a rented body." In *Close to the Knives*, he reflects on "renting" his life: "Ever since I was a kid I couldn't shake the realization that life was essentially a series of activities designed so that one could pay out money to keep from dying; if one stopped paying, one died." His work remains shocking, enraging, bereaved, and unforgettably beautiful. Reading him, looking at his artwork, offers nothing *useful*, but it's a shove into a disorienting emotional landscape you never forget.

***

It is the spatial imagination that maps our mythographies, our victimographies—that imposes or suggests any kind of confinement to an identity, whether we want to belong to it or not. It is the spatial imagination that commodifies human beings and replaces them with lifestyles—that, in other words, gentrifies a person by replacing them with a consumer-category. It is what suggests, coerces, or polices how one should look, act, buy, and live. Obviously, as I've tried to relate with the way music is consumed, these facile, consumer-friendly categories aren't limited to ideas we're supposed to fear or denigrate: they can work their way into every aspect of our lives, even those we enjoy—or need—most.

Kimberlé Crenshaw's theory of intersectionality, for example—which looks to the ways socioeconomic and political oppression can intersect with gender discrimination—is one of the most useful, powerful, and empathetic philosophies for thinking against oppression; and yet many well-intentioned people seem to use it as a way to graph their identities on a matrix—to point at a hierarchy and say, *I am here*. Once commodified like this, intersectionality can begin to seem competitive, a quest to recognize the "most marginalized," which is antithetical to using one's overlapping privileges—even as a marginalized person—to protest, lobby, and legislate toward a less oppressive society.

That theories like Crenshaw's are reduced and demeaned is not because of human stupidity or oversimplification, but co-optation, or the overwhelming assimilative power of capitalist consumerism. Those who misuse political -isms and -alities, even out of good will, tend to denigrate, devalue, or ignorantly pollute these terms until they mean little or nothing, neutralizing their anti-capitalist power. To be intersectional, in this naïvely co-opted language, starts to sound as if one shops at many different stores to supplement one's variety of overlapping identities. As it goes with art, this diluting of critical, even revolutionary ideas is a gentrification of politics, whereby a consumable image of an idea, a historical event, or a political belief replaces the real-life complexity of that idea or event or belief. And ours, it's no surprise, is an unbearably gentrified era of political thinking.

To take an annual example from Pride celebrations across the country: Who decides what a group of queer individuals should *look* like? How do other queers intuit what is appropriate and what is not? Every year, a small subset of the LGBTQ+ community voices its displeasure over fetish gear and other "hypersexual" outfits at Pride celebrations, often likening it to sexual assault or child sexual abuse. In 2019, Matthew J. Phillips, a writer and literature professor, spoke out against these complaints: "To argue—falsely—that [seeing BDSM gear] is a violation of your consent is to argue that the public sphere must be policed and certain expressions of behavior and sexuality excluded," Phillips wrote. The argument in favor of "respectability politics" at Pride events is quintessential, Phillips says, of the "cis-hetero-patriarchy"—a powerful social apparatus that legislates what is normal and what is not among sexuality and expression.

It's similarly depressing, to say the least, to see LGBTQ+ individuals using children as rhetorical props, since an imagined threat to children has been, for centuries, the easiest way to convince the public to dehumanize queer people.

This heteronormative impulse—this othering of LGBTQ+ persons by their own peers—is not isolated to arguments over sexual expression. Witnessing a parallel behavior is, after all, what led Schulman to write *Gentrification of the Mind*. In late 2010, Schulman met with several young queer artists who were curious about the AIDS Coalition to Unleash Power (ACT UP). Instrumental in publicizing AIDS as a crisis, the members of ACT UP "had created change through confrontation, alienation, and truth telling," and had found admirers among this new generation of queer artists. Still, these younger artists' "professional instincts led them in different directions: accommodation, social positioning, even unconscious maneuvering." In other words, this new generation had "depoliticized" and "depersonalized" their queer experiences. Like many young queer people—and like I had done when I'd decided, long ago, to avoid referring to myself in professional settings

CF. P85   as a gay or queer artist—they had internalized the "normalcy" of queerness in mass culture, including entertainment and advertising, which allowed them to forget the more radical and consequential elements of queer history, as well as hide or soften any high-register queer representation within their own work or public life.

Schulman's metaphor for this thinking is gentrification. By erasing "complexity, difference, dynamic, dialogic action for change," she argues, gentrification becomes "a kind of institutionalization of culture," and identity becomes a commodity. The metaphor is apt, especially in a country whose mythology intimates that anything can be bought, even a new life. In cities, gentrification is what happens to neighborhoods when they no longer resemble what made us want to, or able to, live there. Those who live happily in gentrified neighborhoods patronize the same establishments one finds in gentrified areas nationwide. Luxury apartments built over demolished, once-affordable housing resemble those in other cities, filled with furniture and décor from the same retailers. Bars, restaurants, clubs, arcades, and breweries siphon activity from public spaces, which go neglected and underfunded. The densest and busiest urban spaces in America assume the trappings of suburbs, even gated communities.

Key to gentrification is replacement. Those who seek the neighborhoods described above seek suburban comfort in an urban environment, with people of color and those living in poverty placed at a distance via private transit (personal cars and ride-sharing apps), pricing (tickets and cover charges), and aggressive policing. This is not how a person is meant to live in a city; but, in photographs, it certainly looks as if one is living in a city. Gentrification is the replacement of city living with an image of city living, often informed by social media or entertainment. It is performing, for one's own benefit, a consumer identity—city dweller—at the expense of a neighborhood that other people once called home.

Just as replacing urban life with an image of urban life is an act of gentrification that affects vulnerable persons, so too is the replacement of lived queer sexuality with a consumer image (rainbows, nuclear units, "love is love") a parallel harm. Those left out of the image of what palatable queerness looks like are often poor, people of color, trans, and so on. Schulman isn't the only one to see this connection. Writing for *Harper's* in January of 2018, Fenton Johnson observed how "The evolution from ACT UP and Zen Hospice to state-sanctioned marriage is precisely analogous to gentrification—the creative outliers do the heavy lifting, and when a certain level of safety has been achieved, the assimilationists move in, raise prices, and force out the agents of change." Standing with a clipboard and asking strangers to "legalize love," a young person can assume the image of a political activist. But championing marriage as the solution to bigotry erases a more radical history in which a neglected, marginalized community "insisted," in Johnson's words, "that *we* had something to offer, that *our* world, where we formed enduring relationships outside the tax code and the sanction of the church and state, where we created and took care of families of lovers and friends and strangers alike . . . was richer, more sustainable, and more loving."

Instead of this queer alternative to an institution entrenched in property rights, the movement to legalize gay marriage retreats into a reduced, simplified image: The queer family is identical to the heterosexual family. And with that image, what was once queer and radical capitulates to the same capitalist hierarchy that, only thirty years ago, watched tens of thousands of LGBTQ+ people suffer and die, often alone, because they were different. And with this new image of the safe, wholesome queer couple or family, we also have new differences. Families, so pictured, are not trans, they are not polyamorous, they are rarely Black or Indigenous or Latinx, and—at least in advertisements—they are certainly not poor.

As this process continues within queer politics, so too are all political ideas vulnerable to gentrification. This shouldn't be a surprise in a country where socialism is still often discussed in the narrow terms of a specifically totalitarian species of Communism, nor in a country where identity politics is misconstrued and then swatted back and forth among septuagenarian politicians and pundits like a shuttlecock.

To use simplified or flattened images in place of a more nuanced, complex reality is an isolating, ignorant approach to both the past and the present, and confronts us with a significant threat. In a word, that threat is fascism. Historical fascist movements—including Mussolini's capital-F original—often arose to "protect" land and factory owners, i.e., the gentry, from proletarian revolutions. Fascism is a politics that guards the privileged from those they oppress. A violent and autocratic perversion of populism, fascism is the apotheosis of gentrified politics: its promises, ideas, and policies are almost totally cleaved from reality—images all.

Before his death in 2014, the political philosopher Ernesto Laclau observed that populist movements, whether from the left or the right, are predicated on an "idea of a fullness which unfulfilled demands constantly reproduce as the presence of an absence." There is no meeting fascist demands because these demands are never clear; they are inevitably framed outside of the present, disseminating a nostalgic image of the nation's past or a "perfection of man" in some unreachable future. There is no "great" America to restore into being, only an image gentrified by decades of political rhetoric and popular entertainment. When our national politics is replaced by a gallery of images—"Main Street versus Wall Street," "illegal" immigrants, latte-sipping cosmopolitans, the "white working class," coastal elites, hardworking Christian families, and so on—that politics becomes irreconcilable with reality. Yet, voted into office, our senators and representatives, our governors and presidents, use these images to inform policy decisions that affect the real lives of their constituents. And one only has to look to Flint or to Ferguson, to trans women murdered in our cities or to the concentration camps at the southern border, to understand how, through inaction, neglect, or corruption, our elected officials often affect those lives by ending them.

It is because of gentrified thinking that fascism in the United States is not only possible but, for four years, could rule from the White House. The American taste for commodifying ideas and identities—of shelving nearly everything that can be thought or believed in a market of interchangeable, consumable images—has all but welcomed it. Because once the fascist imagination acquires the strength of the state, the state begins replacing reality with its promised, simple, easily grasped image of that nation, eliminating whatever doesn't fit within its frame: notably, human beings.

Talent was blazing through the columns and
onto the coffee tables. The physical-assault
metaphors had taken over the reviews . . .
'Gut-busting' and 'gut-wrenching' were ac-
colades. 'Nerve-shattering,' 'eye-popping,'
'bone-crunching'—the responsive critic
was a crushed, impaled, electrocuted man.

—RENATA ADLER, *Speedboat*

The imagination of gentrification is also one of cleanness, of
sanitization—which of course, as an imagination, exists on a
scale as wide and varied as "getting rid of garbage left in the
streets" all the way to "getting rid of people who don't look like
us," including the "messiness"
of politics. To the gentrified
neighborhood or belief or work
of art or idea, nothing is added,
only subtracted.

The early twenty-first century vogue for
minimalism is a gentrification of what a lifestyle
looks like—purged of all "excess," including, for
the most part, all color.

In *How to Kill a City*, P. E. Moskowitz details the rapid and
racist degradation of neighborhoods into unlivable real estate store-

houses. Gentrification, they write, is "a void in a neighborhood, in a city, in a culture. In that way, gentrification is a trauma, one caused by the influx of massive amounts of capital into a city and the consequent destruction following in its wake." Contrary to the myth of "gentrifiers," Moskowitz clarifies that "gentrification is not about individual acts" but finds its roots in "systemic violence based on decades of racist housing policy in the United States" as well as "a political system focused more on the creation and expansion of business opportunity than on the well-being of its citizens." Ultimately, "gentrification is a system that places the needs of capital (both in terms of city budget and in terms of real estate profits) above the needs of the people." Gentrification trains citizens—through consumerism, relocation, and the myth of agency—to see differently, to spend differently, and, most importantly, to civically engage differently (usually by aligning themselves with police rather than their neighbors).

But gentrification also happens outside of cities. In Olivia Laing's meditation on art and isolation, *The Lonely City*, she recalls sleeping in a room off Times Square, now "populated by Disney characters and tourists and scaffolders and the police." Laing imagines none other than Wojnarowicz, a spirit from an older New York, inhabiting a previous Times Square, its hotels full of "rotting mattresses and doors sawed two feet from the floor, so that any creep could crawl in while you slept," and, outside, "the panhandlers, the hustlers, the damaged and hungry bodies." Laing doubts the gentrification of New York was in any way "driven by a wish to improve or make safe the lives of people on the margins." Instead, rhetoric demanding "safer cities, cleaner cities, richer cities, cities that grow ever more alike" is borne of "a profound fear of difference, a fear of dirt and contamination, an unwillingness to let other life-forms coexist. And what this means is that cities shift from places of contact, places where diverse people interact, to places that resemble isolation wards." The pain of others becomes unclean; poverty and suffering must be swept from the streets in order for money to be spent happily. In ourselves, too, loneliness and discomfort must be medicated and controlled: "Amidst the glossiness of late capitalism, we are fed the notion that all difficult feelings—depression, anxiety, loneliness, rage—are simply a consequence of unsettled chemistry, a problem to be fixed, rather than a response to structural injustice." If we deny others the right to express their suffering, we deny it to ourselves: our unmet needs and aspirations scar over into shame that only transactions can keep hidden.

The "uncleanness" of suffering might be why photography is the preferred window to the pain of others. Just as seeing attained even more cultural dominance during the COVID-19 pandemic, the primacy of sight establishes a safe and visible distance between people in pain and the people who, politically, have a hand in causing it. One's pain cannot contaminate the other.

***

Against difficult emotions, the gentrified imagination distrusts the body, from which the deepest, most difficult, least neatly labeled emotions tend to bubble up. Few today, from a scientific perspective, would seriously argue the Cartesian schism. Yet in a great deal of discourse—particularly on art—the sincerity of the body is disingenuously absent. Even in its most cerebral, image-distant forms (such as literature), art has the capacity to provoke bodily responses. Some of these are acknowledged—adrenaline, with respect to horror; tears, with respect to melodramas—while others are kept secret. While he may lament his "shattered nerves," no critic would mention the very real erection inching across his lap during an arousing scene in a film or novel that's supposed to be serious.

The most bodily feelings—sexual—reveal, in the lingering suspicion of pornography among critics and artists, just how gentrified even theater and cinema—even literature—have become. Like the most ecstatic experiences with art, pornography—good pornography—excites passions that anticipate reasoning. Something deeply emotional within the body is made palpable via the intellect's abandonment of its pretensions, its expectations. Of its control over the experience of the experience.

The most privately consumed of all arts, pornography promises a self-transcendence relatively unimpeded by cultural frameworks that reinforce images of *how a person like you should be*—at least until it's no longer private. The shame built up around pornography is not exclusive to its sexual acts or imagined partners. A video clip watched alone may bring undiluted ecstasy (literally: "out of place"), but bring a friend into it, even someone to jerk off with, and that same clip becomes ridiculous: the dialogue laughable, each moan an embarrassment. Watching porn with a friend, one surveils oneself as a consumer—a triangulation we perform automatically, especially the more visible we become as consumers. Should you become dislodged from the mythographical coordinates in which capitalism has mapped you and your behaviors, it no longer knows how to sell to you. To understand you as a market, capitalism must reduce you, eliminating not only what's extraneous but what is transgressive from your life and personality. *This kind of porn*, capitalism trains your friends and lovers to say, *just isn't you*. It selects against your complexity, your multitudes.

Enjoyed privately, porn is the most transgressive art there is in capitalist and fascist societies, which is precisely why, alongside queerness, it is targeted by authoritarians. If nothing else, porn's sheer plenitude, especially its amateur contributions, illustrate just how many people there are in the world who love sex and aren't ashamed to show themselves loving it. I think of this when I scroll through an inexhaustible supply of images, all these men across the world who display themselves with men, for men, and how they've taught me nearly everything I know about sex—its kinks, its dynamics, even its anatomical mechanics. Like any art, porn has the capacity to enlarge life. It embraces pluralistic and contradictory experiences of the world.

Yes, porn has its own myths, many of which are reductive, even harmful, but here is where its quality and its ethics are important. Just as classical theater, realist novels, and the Hollywood blockbuster excel when they "cross into new territory"—i.e., when they escape genre—pornography is at its best when it leaves the masquerade of masc and femme behind, when characters become *authentic*, when the actors convince us that what is felt is genuinely felt (even if it's not). The transcendence we come to seek in porn is of human beings appearing to experience unregulated, unchecked, ungentrified, and even unobserved pleasure, an authenticity that mirrors the "realism" of character or action in other, less controversial forms of art.

Maybe it shouldn't surprise us, then, that the word "god" is more common in porn than in scripture. Experiences of self-transcendence, of ecstasy, are imagined as being face-to-face with god, as stepping outside of this world to meet god, where god may simply be our word for looking directly at the self—the deep, unsocialized self. Like cherished art, great porn dramatizes the human experience of the self looking at the self, of what is possible when all that is social, cultural, and historical is seared away. It shows us the possibility, but never the proof, of what our vocabulary can only call a soul. Without risking this kind of vulnerability, it's almost impossible to see the violence in the most unsolicited image there is: a civilization predicated on imprisoning these radiant selves behind masks, on blocking out each individual's light.

The frequency with which we resort to religious metaphors to describe extreme states of consciousness has introduced a ruthlessly limiting cynicism into art and art criticism. Even in this book, filling itself with souls, faith, ecstasy—mentioning, even, *cathedrals* that art seems to carve out from the fleshy interiors of our bodies, creating a kind of *sanctuary*—it's hard for me not to feel ashamed. Yet just because I don't believe in God doesn't mean I can't want there to be something like it.

***

It's the wanting that's important, the sense that this something should be there, or perhaps, even, that it *is* there. The religious or spiritual impulse is a craving for unverified, unverifiable knowledge, even if we know that knowledge, or feel it, to be right or real. This is why so much art, even the most fantastical, fictional stories, feel true. Art and experiences like it beckon the call of the conscience.

A person's conscience is their "with-knowledge" within, a sensibility that can be developed or demeaned over time, depending on how often one listens to its call. Conscience, according to Heidegger, discloses: "If we analyse conscience more penetratingly, it is revealed as a *call*. Calling is a mode of *discourse*. The call of conscience has the character of an *appeal* to Dasein [one's own 'Being-there'] by calling it to its own most potentiality-for-Being-Self; and this is done by way of *summoning* it to its own most Being-guilty." Why guilty?

Speaking of conscience, I'm aware of Heidegger's notorious politics—namely, his collaboration with the Nazis as they swept through German universities, which is not only unconscionable but mysterious. That is, there's a darkness between Heidegger's written moral clarity w/r/t the conscience, the inner life, the soul, and the moral failure of his actions. That a person can articulate so richly and magnetically (that is, so frustratingly *unclearly*) the inner workings of the conscience and ignore their own is, at the very least, a warning.

Unlike shame, guilt recognizes action from being: it accepts time as a potential source of change, rather than confining one's identity in the permanence of imagined space. Shame *is*; guilt is *right now*. A person is guilty because of their actions—what they've said, what they've done, even what they've thought. Often, these actions are at odds with that person's belief in who they "really" are—"who I am deep down," "who I've always been," and so on. "To the call of conscience," Heidegger goes on, "there corresponds a possible hearing. Our understanding of the appeal unveils itself as our *wanting to have a conscience*." One wants, in other words, to be guided, even if by one's own innermost self or life or voice or soul, or—if not—by some outward manifestation of that same moral compass, be it God, an ideology, a practice, a relationship with the natural world, a belief system, or—it should be said—be it an easily understood, omnipresent, abusive bigot who tells you everything is going to be okay if you just support him unconditionally, unquestioningly.

Dasein (again, one's own "Being-there") is an entity "which has been thrown." For Heidegger, thrown-ness is a kind of separation from the inner life: "'*Being*-thrown' means finding oneself in some state of mind or other. One's state-of-mind is therefore based upon thrownness." The conscience, then, is the call back—the plea to return. The state of mind of the self has, perhaps, taken too much of its surroundings or environs into itself. In the vocabulary of this book, the self understands itself as an image, as fixed space. Heidegger calls this the "they-self"—the assimilation of what others say, what others believe, what others want, into one's own consciousness: "Dasein, as a Being-with which understands, can *listen* to Others. Losing itself in the publicness and the idle talk of the 'they,' it *fails to hear* its own Self in listening to the they-self." To rectify this with a call of conscience, with a return to a focus—a grasp—upon the inner life, Dasein "must first be able to find itself—to find itself as something which has failed to hear itself, and which fails to hear in that it *listens away* to the 'they.' This listening-away must get broken off . . . The possibility of another kind of hearing which will interrupt it, must be given by Dasein itself." The person who wants to listen to their conscience—the person who wishes to develop the sensibility (and sensitivity) of the conscience—will place themselves at risk of experiences that may provoke the call. These experiences—art, religious relationships, intense sexual contact or fantasies, hallucinogens, psychotic episodes, extreme terror, and great jokes—are all bodily experiences; they aim themselves at what we will feel before we understand it.

These impressions, which Edmund Burke identifies as "whatever is fitted in any sort to excite the ideas of pain and danger," must remain at a distance in order to feel sublime. They are, he writes, "delightful when we have an idea of pain and danger, without being actually in such circumstances." The sublime "anticipates our reasonings, and hurries us on by an irresistible force."

One seeks these experiences because they are unique and intense, and often in some inexplicable way reaffirming: "In understanding the call, Dasein is *in thrall to its own most possibility of existence.* It has chosen itself." Later, Heidegger likens this call of conscience to "care": in developing our sensibility, our conscientiousness, we care for ourselves.

It isn't the right word, but no one "understands" this like David Lynch, the most visible director whose films are not only popular but resistant works of art. That is, they wrap themselves around a provocative darkness and demand, relentlessly, that the viewer's Dasein call to itself. In *Twin Peaks*, for example, the Black and White Lodges seem to be the realm of what must be art. Though dressed for a hike, Dale Cooper enters the waiting room in his impeccable black suit. Laura Palmer, first seen in the series as a pale, sand-flecked corpse, wears an elegant dress. The waiting room itself—furnished with black leather chairs and art deco lamps—is the antithesis of the town's northwestern kitsch of mounted fish, knickknacks, overstuffed sofas, and overwhelming plaid. Instead of the haunted fifties bop of the diner's jukebox, the Black Lodge features a soundtrack of slow, dark jazz with vocals by the otherworldly Jimmy Scott. Here is the *Venus de' Medici*; in the hallway, the *Venus de Milo*. The curtains conjure a stage.

Simply being in the Lodge indicates that one is both participating in and witnessing some kind of performance, where conversation, spoken backward and reversed to create a doppelgänger of English, becomes a script.

Lynch's work holds a special magnetism for moths like me—those drawn to darkness, to what cannot be seen. His strobe-lit hallways, shadows, emotional juxtapositions, and uncanny doubles are cinema's imposing Rothkos—the macchia, to return to Imbriani's word, that excites our passions. Often, our emotional relationship with such art is an imaginary or extradimensional room of its own—one we don't know how we've entered, one we don't know when we'll leave. In *The Doubles*—a passionate, genre-dismantling memoir told

Again, Lynch's aesthetics and erotics seem aimed at the inner life Heidegger describes: "The caller [of conscience] is Dasein in its uncanniness: primordial, thrown Being-in-the-world as the 'not-at-home'—the bare 'that-it-is' in the 'nothing' of the world. The caller is unfamiliar to the everyday they-self."

through film criticism—Veronica Esposito likens this space to the subconscious. Cinema, in particular, has a "unique gift" for piercing one's core: "If music is the most euphoric art, literature the most contemplative, and painting the most prophetic, then film," she writes, "is the most psychological. It crashes through the bottom of the soul and forces a reckoning with those long-hidden things."

This question of the soul is an undercurrent in Esposito's book. Contemplating Krzysztof Kieślowski's *The Double Life of Véronique*—specifically the director's "trust in mysteries that bend our paths"—she recalls a familiar image: "How many times has it been said that the cineplexes are our civilization's cathedrals? Are these enormous, perfected, glamorized faces not heroes appropriate to a technologically learned humanity?" In dedicating her attention to film, Esposito feels herself "beginning to sketch out the counters of this faith that draws us to the arts. We become ourselves by what deluges us. Humanity is ritualistic, the world is the sum of our rituals."

Faith, ritual, meaning. The soul. While *The Doubles* is restless, the essay on *Véronique*, the film from which Esposito chose her first name, is the book's heart, its axis of being. It is not only where "art tread[s] upon worship's grounds," but where film's power to shape one's artistic sensibilities is most thoroughly explored: "Could any other art form instill the belief in a soul?"

In *Véronique*, a young woman in Kraków, Weronika, falls over dead in the middle of a transcendent vocal performance; the camera pans above the audience "in what can only be the vantage point of the young woman's soul as it departs." From that point on, for Véronique (played by the same actress) in Paris, life loses its joy and direction, its narrative. She quits her music lessons, withdraws from relationships, and loses interest in her young students. Despite—or *because of*—a lack of total understanding, *Véronique*, Esposito says, "opens every last door in my skull. It assures me that life is not the world." Under the film's spell, she finds herself believing in, or at least sensing the existence of, something not only unseen and unproven but unseeable, unprovable. Split into that dual existence, Esposito's double goes where she cannot, a place where reason is subservient to feeling.

One word for this experience is "incantatory."

***

While Sontag was a staunch atheist (she once called herself 200 percent secular), there is from her earliest essays onward an understanding and a nurturing of the spiritual impulse in human beings—of the craving for the "incantatory," to be put under a spell and held there. Shortly before her death, she sat for a televised three-hour interview on CSPAN. To one caller, concerned over George W. Bush's admiration of Christ above all other philosophers, she confessed her ongoing temptation to fortify her moral compass with "one of the great religious traditions." For decades, Sontag engaged the religious imagination and its metaphors—often directly, as in her writings on pornography, silence, and asceticism. The second sentence of *Styles of Radical Will* is a parenthetical definition of spirituality, a word she introduces in the first with scare quotes:

> Every era has to reinvent the project of "spirituality" for itself. (Spirituality = plans, terminologies, ideas of deportment aimed at resolving the painful structural conditions inherent in the human situation, at the completion of human consciousness, at transcendence.)

A great deal of these "painful structural conditions" Sontag attributes to "the capitalist world-view, in which the environment is atomized into 'items' (a category embracing things and persons, works of art and natural organisms), and in which every item is a commodity—that is, a discrete, portable object." It's this attribution that led her to criticize photography itself, its surreal shatteredness as discrete and portable pieces of the world. The photographer collects what they see—an extension of the colonial, capitalist imagination.

We are psychically wounded, in a sense, by our confinement into categories; and our poor attempts at healing—bad pornography, mediocre art, a reliance upon religious metaphors, and so on—reflect "the traumatic failure of modern capitalist society to provide authentic outlets for the perennial human flair for high-temperature visionary obsessions, to satisfy the appetite for exalted self-transcending modes of concentration and seriousness. The need of human beings to transcend 'the personal' is no less profound than the need to be a person." To transcend the self, we often seek "total" experiences, which "tend again and again to be

apprehended only as revivals or translations of the religious imagination. To try to make a fresh way of talking at the most serious,
ardent, and enthusiastic level, heading off the religious encapsu-
lation, is one of the primary intellectual tasks of future thought."
Even today—especially today—there remains very little room, in
language, for the sublime or divine apart from the debris of harmful, often oppressive institutions; even contemporary attempts
at spirituality are quickly poisoned by slogans, marketing, social
media, and cultural colonialism—"mindfulness," for example, or
"being present," or a white suburbanite evangelizing their latest
journey into savasana.

Introducing her ideas on pornography, Sontag mentions the
relationship between the deadpan and slapstick in comedy, both
of which produce "a deadening or neutralization or distancing of
the audience's emotions." So too does this apply in conventional
porn: "The principles of underrating and frenetic agitation make
the emotional climate self-canceling, so that the basic tone of
pornography is affectless, emotionless." Porn, like comedy, is in-
terminable in spirit, "a perpetual tableau. Even though things do
happen, really nothing happens. Everything is repeated." There are
no consequences because there is no suffering, there is no change.
She contrasts this with tragedy, in which "we believe in the reality
of suffering. We believe in the reality of death."

These are distinctions worth observing: there is something we
seek in comedy and in pornography that tragedy does not, perhaps
cannot, provide. But, as with any consumption, there are risks. A
contemporary risk of this sensibility is—again—found in social
media, particularly as it intersects, even enmeshes itself, with the
news cycle.

The surrealist ethos of social media, wherein an image of a
mass shooting is structurally equivalent with the image of a friend
announcing a new job, replicates exactly the kind of ongoing, in-

terminable "frenetic agitation" and deadpan lack of response one finds in Sontag's characterizations of comedy and pornography. This was especially apparent with the forty-fifth presidential administration, whose ongoing spectacle, amplified and magnified by social media, left its audience both incredulous and numb. In life under a Trump presidency, nothing changes. Despite the daily threat of apocalypse, each day is almost identical to any other. Caught between affectlessness and total, constant hysteria, it's difficult to even pretend one can feel like oneself when using these platforms, and yet—participating as one does as an image—that self is increasingly confined. Sometimes seriously, sometimes jokingly, but always honestly, we call this space of confinement a "brand."

Here, again, is a technology or sensibility that offers a glimpse of transcending the personality or escaping the capitalist atomization; and yet it withholds that possibility. It fails us. Social media platforms are built for advertisers; they are profit-generating machines, just like the conventional pornography and formulaic, socially narcotic comedy Sontag describes. This, again, is the "traumatic failure of modern capitalism," as well as its unique ability to assimilate as a visible commodity nearly everything it encounters. We still have few outlets, little language, and only the rare subversive system of thought to provide or pursue an ancient and necessary spirituality. We have little left outside the realm of transactions. We are losing what is "sacred."

***

In his *Confessions*, Augustine recalls losing a close friend at a young age. This is prior to his ascetic relationship with God, at a moment in his life when his habits, patterns, and supports were crumbling: "Whither should my heart flee from my heart? Whither should I flee from myself? Whither not follow myself?" Ultimately, it's

Like Heidegger's Dasein, Augustine wants to be guided, and places this desire—let's call it his soul—in the imagined heart of Christ, which, by the grace of Augustine's own will, guides (or pulls) Augustine forward through life.

only in God's truth—in the "perfect man" of Christ—that Augustine finds his peace: "Our heart is restless, until it repose in Thee."

The sincerity of Augustine's gratitude is palpable, enviable. For most of my adult life, I've never perceived or allowed myself to have a soul. It's difficult to read these *Confessions* and not crave Augustine's assurance that there is something beyond the body's chemistry of neurons and amines, its meat and memory. Of course, this is why one believes—why I believe—so adamantly in the necessity of art, and why another might believe in the necessity of meditation, and why a third might find it spiritually crucial to cause and prolong unbearable suffering in others—even those they've never met—in order to "save" them.

So too do our societal phrases—"Thank God"; "Bless you"; "God willing"—make me cringe when they automatically leave my lips. Like a militant idiot, I repent when I say them, as if I've sinned against language. This cynicism limits the creation of art as well as one's capacity for experiencing it as totally, as ecstatically, as possible.

As an atheist, I've shied away from "soul" for so long that to say it sincerely feels transgressive. But what kind of idiot resists the extraordinary gift of having, and claiming, a soul? In most languages, "soul" is derived from the breath or breathing, the air pushed in and out of the body; it is the soul that, as the Greeks imagined, gives wings to our words. In *Véronique*, this breath is everywhere: condensing on mirrors and windows, heaved out of her body during sex, wrenched out while grieving, and, above all, pushed through her lungs to make music it's hard to believe any human body can make. In fact, one might envision that Weronika, onstage in her first and final performance, pushed that soul too hard, that she sang it right out of her body.

But the soul is also light. As Véronique wakes from a nap, a glow flitting across her face, she goes to the window and sees a boy with a mirror, teasing her from a neighboring balcony. She smiles; he and his mirror retreat into his own apartment. "So easily does the sensation of an invisible world dissolve," Esposito remarks, but when Véronique turns back inside, the light remains—"dancing in the corner." As she approaches it,

> the shot changes: we are looking down at her . . . As though seized with a premonition Véronique jerks her head up, she stares into the camera. It tilts in response. The realization is immediate. It's a point of view shot. I'm seeing from the point of view of that yellow light. Which can of course only be the point of view of Weronika . . . Every other mystery in *Véronique* has some explanation. But not this one. There is no source for the second light.

Depicting the soul as breath or light: These are ancient metaphors fossilized in language. Yet we don't seem to tire of them. In *Twin Peaks: The Return*, Carl Rodd witnesses the hit-and-run killing of a young boy. As the boy's mother screams for help, Rodd sees a blur of light lift out of his body and ascend into the clouds. The soul floating up to heaven: the stuff of *Looney Tunes*, and yet in Lynch's hands, so masterful one doesn't know whether to grieve or rejoice.

So, too, at the end of *Fire Walk with Me*, when Laura Palmer meets her angel in the waiting room. Instead of cringing at this cliché, one is overcome with a feeling of immense grief, and of gratitude. Witnessing Palmer's joy—sobs that turn into laughter—is one of the most inexplicably moving experiences I've had in front of a screen. In what is possibly the greatest triumph of the human CF. P100 imagination over its animal chemistry, it makes me unafraid of death. Reposing there, my heart is at rest.

***

After praising the "incantatory" power of art, Sontag, in one of her earliest essays, creates a critical binary: "In place of a hermeneutics we need an erotics of art." Perhaps inevitably, art is taught at the grade school and university levels as a system of codes, as a language neat with definitions. What does the whale signify, in *Moby-Dick*? What does Velázquez's placement of the king and queen say about the Spanish monarchy? What are these books and paintings and films and photographs *really about*? It's this obsession with aboutness, in the hermeneutical tradition, that seems inseparable from art itself—that speaks art, whereas art itself seems silent.

Sontag's alternative would function quite differently: "What is important now is to recover our senses. We must learn to see more, to hear more, to feel more . . . The function of criticism should be to show how it is what it is, even that it is what it is, rather than to show what it means." Sontag challenges the critic to embrace the ecstasy of trying to satisfy an insurmountable desire to understand. Hermes, the messenger god, decrypted Olympian mysteries so that humankind could understand. To channel Eros—child of Love and War—is to lose control over one's language. An erotics is a celebration of art's power to knock us dumb.

Erotic theory is a visualization of desire, of the path or circuit desire takes. An experience of desire is a contradiction in time, in selfhood, and in language—so much so that Sappho, as Anne Carson writes, coined a new word: "The moment when the soul parts on itself in desire is conceived as a dilemma of body and senses. On Sappho's tongue, as we have seen, it is a moment of bitter and sweet . . . Boundaries of body, categories of thought, are confounded." This anticipation of reasoning applies not only to love but to the pursuit of knowledge, of experiences, of life, and of art: "In letters as in love, to imagine is to address oneself to what is not." Without desire, there is no struggle against time. To want for CF. P145 nothing is to float as flotsam in time's river until your life is washed out to sea and forgotten.

In *Eros the Bittersweet*, Carson describes an unstable triangulation of seeing: "Writing about desire, the archaic poets made triangles with their words. Or, to put it less sharply, they represent situations that ought to involve two factors (lover, beloved) in terms of three (lover, beloved and the space between them, however realized)." Desire itself opens up a new dimension: what should be a simple connection between two points is complicated by a third. That third dimension—the space between lover and beloved, reader and text, audience and artwork—is what destabilizes a flat, orderly, linear universe.

This is art, a rupture in space—the very instability of which demands its closure as quickly as possible. Here is where that effort to interpret comes from, or to explain, to name, to categorize, to pull back the curtain, to reduce this magic to smoke and mirrors. The universe is torn and seeks to sew itself shut. With art, something inexplicable, yet magnetic, is happening, and as long as it exists—as long as the spell of it lingers—there is not only our world as we understand it but our world *and* whatever this is, whatever's out there defying all we know. It's the mark of a long-lasting work of art to keep that unstable space open, dangerous, exciting, uninterpretable.

Without interpretation, there is no language. An experience of art we don't understand is not "like" anything we've seen. In fact, there's something about it we're not seeing—no other half to reach for and pull close until what is delightful becomes banal, ready-made, repeatable. Our words are left unfinished.

Where Eros reigns, Hermes cannot follow. The ruptures art tears open are dark. Experiences of desire, as Carson points out, are terrible; its metaphors are of "war, disease and bodily dissolution." For these poets, "Change of self is loss of self." To desire is to melt or collapse, to blend or break. The boundaries of self—and the body imagined alongside it—are violated; there is no longer a skin to point to, in a sense, that shields whatever "you" are from whatever the rest of us, or the world, may be.

In contemporary life, where more of what is tangible is retreating into a digital dimension of its own, to fall under art's spell may become increasingly important—and, in certain capacities, increasingly dangerous. There are people—me included—who find great pleasure in being so changed, so destroyed. *Twin Peaks*, for example, is without a doubt my *Véronique*—the closest experience I've had to believing in something resembling a soul. Like the Black and White Lodges depicted in its universe, it opens a space within me, a cavernous sanctuary wherein I feel safe, expansive, limitless, loved. This does not mean, of course, that I imagine myself—or that anyone experiencing a work of art imagines oneself—within the universe or realm depicted; only an idiot would "feel safe" in *Twin Peaks*. This is not what I mean by the opening of space. Instead, what is between me and *Twin Peaks* is a field of great tension, and it's this tension which opens something new, that charges itself like a great energy field, that gathers to itself an unfathomable gravity, like a singularity, and which offers me some place to hide or leave a part of myself—if not forever, for as long as the portal, let's call it, is open. For as long as the singularity, let's call it, pulls and bends my light toward it.

And there are people—again, me included—who make it their life's ambition to similarly tear such holes in the universe, who wish always to remind others of the unseeable and unknowable, the unnameable.

Unfortunately, this same magnetism applies to aesthetic projects which employ erotic tension (that is, which *seduce*) without an ethical compass—or those which deliberately smash that compass. Benjamin, in the 1930s, wrote that "the logical result of Fascism is the introduction of aesthetics into politics." It is, he said, a political system that gives "the masses not their right, but instead a chance to express themselves." Even Goebbels himself reflected that politics was "the highest and most comprehensive art." To mention erotics in combination with fascism, especially National Socialism, usually refers to the eroticized aesthetics of fascism. But the true seductive power of fascism is not aesthetic at all, no matter how eroticized these aesthetics may be. In fact, these aesthetics hide fascism's vast and absolute erotic intensity—its capacity to unendingly withhold release or relief or satisfaction from every single one of its believers.

Populism, writes Ernesto Laclau, "requires the dichotomic division of society into two camps—one presenting itself as a part which claims to be the whole." On a political level, this is the field of tension Carson describes—the imagined completeness of one "camp" frustrated by seeing its own incompleteness reflected back. In the populist crowd, especially the fascist crowd, "there is the experience of a *lack*, a gap which has emerged in the harmonious continuity of the social. There is a fullness of the community which is missing. This is decisive: the construction of the 'people' will be the attempt to give a name to that absent fullness." Fascism is a political art that wraps itself around darkness, that pulls its believers inward and intensifies their desire for "order" (death) and "greatness" (destruction) by ever prolonging, delaying, and denying that desire. Fascist theater is a masterpiece of erotic art, and—as we've seen—one of the most dangerous works of art there is.

Of the practice of art, including experiences as total and as deadly as fascism, what I think is that we are all looking for places to leave these pieces of ourselves, and that it's somehow imperative to us that we don't understand where these places come from, nor even, with any predictability, where to find them. What I think is that we are all looking to fill what is dark—what is terrifying, what is delightful, what is sublime—with the immense, inexhaustible light of our souls. Whereas Heidegger imagined one's consciousness as "thrown" and that the conscience calls it back, what I think is that one's conscience *throws the soul*—into art, into religious experiences, into sex, into whatever ecstasy translates for us—and the call is that which calls us forward. This, I think, is why poets create words, why social media users make memes, why lonely people write books: we drag ourselves through time by throwing our souls forward, by projecting them into ideas or experiences that hold us under the intensity of their spells, and we then imagine they call us, beckon us. And when the magic is over, we cast these souls into something new.

Creation is how we allow ourselves the experience of time without the trauma of seeing it as space. It is how, in Azoulay's terminology, we watch ourselves as we live, and how we teach ourselves to watch others as they live alongside us.

IV

THE "RESISTANCE" AND OTHER STORIES

W e need writers," Jennifer Egan wrote for *Time* at the end of 2018, "and we need them badly. Literature, like democracy, is built of a plurality of ideas . . . By writing and reading, we remind ourselves of the value of empathy, subtlety and contradiction." It's an easy wish to understand: that by the assumed virtue of writing, some truth is attained, an elemental and unignorable human compassion.

I love Egan's work, but her portrayal of the writer in America is a fantasy. A writer, in reality, has the same duty to feel as superfluous and humiliated as anyone else caught in this country's downward spiral of cultural and economic decline. Writers write, and if they're lucky they publish in magazines and newspapers and books—an industrial model equally subject to the realities of American capitalism. That is, equally in decline.

While Egan's defense arrives in terrifying times, it creates just as much of an "opioid effect" to believe in the image of the writer as it does to feverishly share the image of an incompetent, cruel president. If writers were the solution, or even part of it, a white nationalist would've never made it past his first primary: America is rich in writers, and always has been.

To put it another way, it's increasingly laughable to be called necessary in a culture with fewer and fewer places to even approach with ideas, much less hope to sell them. American culture—even American literary culture—does not revere its writers. With few exceptions, our writers are less the province of ideas or guidance than they are a container for aspiration: expensive notebooks with pre-printed quotations in the margins, fountain pens, writing programs that cost tens of thousands of dollars, and books that are more enthusiastically instagrammed—that is, visually collected and displayed—than they are read or discussed.

Photographs commit the present to the past, and the idea of the writer in America has long been photographed—an impotently nostalgic romance. It's this romance writers now buy. Like so many other victims of capitalism, writers have been downgraded to a species of consumer. What is expected of us is merely our attention and participation, not our feedback, and never our dissent. Our essays are personal. Our novels are lyrical. The "I" in our poems is the "I" in our profile. Writers are commodities to be bought, hoarded, or sold—and usually on such a niche market that we're mostly buying, hoarding, or selling one another. Clipped of politics and isolated on some pedestal of eternal truth or goodness or empathy, the romanticized, fetishized writer is a disarmed, declawed, defanged writer—little more than someone's rigorously trained pet.

＊

At the turn of the millennium, a novel by a writer who did not exist became an international sensation. "Does it matter," asked *The New York Times*, "that he is 20 years old? That he grew up in West Virginia and later on the streets of San Francisco? That he started publishing at 16, under the pseudonym Terminator?" It shouldn't, the reviewer concluded, "but it does." Only a time traveler could prove it, but JT LeRoy's fame would have likely been impossible without his youth and biography. That his novels were in fact written by a woman fifteen years his senior—that Laura Albert created LeRoy alongside the fiction that wore his name—ultimately proved unpalatable to his fans. Six years after announcing a "deft and imaginative first novel," that same paper exposed LeRoy as a "hoax." In 2002, Albert watched people "bowing down and kneeling before JT" (or Albert's sister-in-law, Savannah Knoop, buried under sunglasses and a blonde wig); but in 2006, "the media came after me, calling me the antichrist." They attacked "with the fury of wasps."

Today, one might say LeRoy was canceled, or at least a version of it. Once adored, his books accumulated single-star ratings on social reading platforms. Worse, as Szilvia Molnar writes in *Literary Hub*, they were forgotten: "The complicated story . . . was reshaped into scandal, and ended up overshadowing the books. There was so much *talking* to and from Albert that *Sarah* and *The Heart Is Deceitful Above All Things* lost their value, their real ability to present as fiction." But even if there is no "JT" to have ostensibly lived their lives, Cherry Vanilla and Jeremiah feel, to the right reader, necessary characters to know. Readers only diminish themselves in getting rid of them, however lied to, however hurt.

"Fiction gets victimized," Molnar went on, "when we try to wring the truth from its authors." In 2019, Zadie Smith interrogated this same imagined idea, "popular in the culture just now," that "we" should stick to characters "who are fundamentally 'like' us: racially, sexually, genetically, nationally, politically, personally." To believe in fiction's ambition to understand the other, or at the very least try to, has become not only passé (Smith fears), but harmful.

As if to confirm this, two writers, shortly before Smith's essay appeared, took issue with fiction's politics—the novel's specifically:

Anne Boyer: "Do novels have bad politics because they are novels?"

Jeet Heer: "The bourgeois mimetic novel limits our political imagination and ability to imagine change. It's going to kill us all."

These critiques of the novel as a form arrived via Twitter, a

CF. P48 medium whose own form is politically dangerous at best, unforgivably apocalyptic at worst. For several days, in a small sphere, these opinions elicited an unusual rage, a niche frustration; yet their implications betray an astounding irresponsibility—not only toward "the novel," but toward literature, toward art, as a human activity. They are, in a word, cynical, which is far more likely to "kill us all" than a mode of fiction. If the "bourgeois novel" limits the political imagination, cynicism eradicates it.

Neither is it helpful that Boyer and Heer never clarified what they meant monolithically by "novels" or "the" novel, which seems to gesture at a British-American, institutionally sanctioned mode—when the "literary" in literary fiction doesn't mean literature so much as a genre in which dogs bark in the distance, parents die of cancer, couples are dishonest with each other, and professors suffer the youth of their students.

We have, Smith claims, *turned away* in our distrust: "In the process of turning from [fiction], we've accused it of appropriation, colonization, delusion, vanity, naïveté, political and moral irresponsibility." Smith, unfortunately, never identifies this "we"—nor those who claim that "only an intimate authorial autobiographical connection with a character can be the rightful basis of a fiction." But the cynicism she senses is, I think, very real. "A performative display of non-interest," she calls it—"a great pride in not being interested in the other, which is sometimes characterized as revenge and sometimes as an act of self-preservation."

It strikes me how many of these same accusations have been leveled at photography, as if the sensibility of the image—mute, spatial, politically slippery, at the mercy of context—were suddenly applicable to long, narrated works of art that create their own contexts.

Cynicism has always attached itself to the personality as rejection. In his *History*, Russell introduces this philosophical milieu, born as Grecian city-states fell to Alexander's empire: "When political power passed into the hands of the Macedonians, Greek philosophers, as was natural, turned aside from politics and devoted themselves more to the problem of individual virtue or salvation." This inward focus, "increasingly subjective and individualistic," laid the groundwork for Christianity's "gospel of individual sal-vation." At last invited to love our neighbors, our neighbors had become politically irrelevant. Their souls passed from citizenship into aesthetics: eternal things no longer worth understanding, only saving. Only collecting. It's no coincidence that Christianity and colonialism are companions, nor that Catholicism is the most image-centric, iconographic of religions.

Today, we are differently conquered, and with different sys-tems of external, impersonal control. Our lives are constantly and overwhelmingly transactional, inflicted with a seemingly in-tentional exhaustion. Cynicism, as a reactionary philosophy, remains—in fact flourishes, ex-pressing itself, Smith writes, "in some version of *I've had enough of, I just can't with*—fill in the blank." It's how "we" cancel, shun, ignore, humiliate, dissociate: our tired and wounded mutila-tions of citizenship, of justice.

> Arendt sees this same exhaustion as a predicate to fascist destruction: "Excluded from participation in the management of public affairs that involve all citizens, the [bourgeois] individual loses his rightful place in society and his natural connection with his fellow-men . . . By assigning his political rights to the state the individual also delegates his social responsibilities to it: he asks the state to relieve him of the burden of caring for the poor precisely as he asks for protection against criminals."

"Fill in the blank" is apt. It implies a single word or short phrase, easily encapsulated, copied, discarded, used. It implies something fixed and shareable, like currency—the function of the image in a visual culture. This is in direct contrast with a project like fiction because, as Smith notes, fiction is "suspicious of any theory of the self that appeared to be largely founded on what can be seen with the human eye." In fiction, the self is a fluid of varying viscosities. It wouldn't make sense to show someone a photograph of a fictional character, not in substitution for their story. Just as we, out here in real life, can't introduce the fullness of ourselves to others with a single image—or even a single social media profile—neither can the characters we meet on the page.

What fiction offers is the representation, or re-creation, of change. "Without an ability to at least guess at what the other might be thinking," Smith writes, "we could have no social lives at all. One of the things fiction did is make this process explicit—visible." In fiction, we can see that lives are in flux, that even stable and consistent identities are fluid. While not as rampant as Smith imagines, if readers turn away from or distrust fiction, they deprive themselves of relatively safe, private, and aesthetically stimulating opportunities to practice seeing other human beings as beings-in-time. This is, I think, why so many scientists tell us that fiction tends to foster empathy in readers: we allow ourselves, from a distance, to allow others their pasts, their mistakes, even their violences—all without turning away.

***

After the 2016 election, when fiction felt not only "more important than ever" but also an escape from noise, I decided to read *Suite Française*—that final, unfinished masterpiece of Irène Némirovsky's. A Ukrainian émigré who found celebrity writing in French in the interwar period, Némirovsky felt tragically, eerily necessary to read.

The *Suite* conjures first a France in chaos as the Reich sweeps through Paris and into the countryside, and later a hushed, claustrophobic France, both tense and indifferent as German soldiers occupy its towns and villages. Némirovsky thrusts her readers into the pandemonium of cities under fire: "Panic-stricken, some of the women threw down their babies as if they were cumbersome packages and ran." One woman, clad in costume jewelry, writhes in agony: "Her throat and fingers were sparkling and blood was pouring from her shattered skull."

All of this, strangely, Némirovsky portrays alongside absurd comedy. The servants of one household, whose "need to follow a routine was stronger than their terror," insist on packing to flee Paris "exactly as they had always done when getting ready to go to the countryside for the summer holidays." These extremes make *Suite Française* the perfect war novel. Rather than poetic or honorable, war is absolute hell (and impossible to replicate in any photograph).

Her most moving pages are those set in provincial France, where the temptation of kindness encourages the French to share their culture with those who seek to destroy it. Despite the German demand for heavier meals, "the French couldn't believe anyone would be crazy enough not to recognise the excellence of their food, especially their golden round loaves, their crown-shaped breads. There were rumours they would soon have to be made with a mixture of bran and poor-quality flour. But no one believed it. They took the German's words as a compliment and were flattered." Naturally, kindness done to power cannot buy kindness in return—only leniency; and even that, as the villagers learn, is never guaranteed.

Call it harrowing, call it absurd, call it tragic, call it brave: *Suite Française*, revealing as it does our psychological incompatibility with life during wartime, is literature par excellence. Yes, it's horrible that people go on gardening and cooking, living laughing loving, while their friends and families are killed, incarcerated, or tortured, while their cities and books burn, but it's also inspiring: we find a way to survive, even if we end up having to lose what it was that made us *us*. We have our tethers to this realest of worlds, no matter what else happens: weather, seasons, food, sensuality. The human ability to adapt is as admirable as it is repulsive.

Némirovsky's work is part of a reading pattern I've developed over the last several years, turning more and more, intentionally or not, to work that confronts the atrocities of fascism, totalitarianism, and ideologies of supremacy—at first intuitively, and later for what would become this book. Many of these books examine or evoke the Second World War, to which it became quite fashionable, in the early days of the Trump presidency, to compare the political arc of the entire contemporary world.

Not that this fashion isn't justified. It's hard not to think of World War II when many Americans have stopped hiding their swastikas, and even fly them proudly. Nor was it hard to make the leap, in one's head, from the rescinding of protections to the proclamation of persecutions, from propaganda to concentration camps—at least until the president built actual concentration camps, and the intuition was no longer necessary.

Familiar, too: our desperation to joke about it all. The renewed popularity of satire when it's almost indistinguishable from reality is another of the twenty-first century's vintage throwbacks. It's easy to grow benumbed to the absurdity of day-to-day life in the United States, where "satire" is simply a reenactment of what happened earlier that week, but with an audience's anesthetic laughter (at least until the physical isolation of the COVID-19 pandemic, where even that went silent). With respect to Trump, the contemporary comedian is barely capable of exaggeration. Aside from expressing genuine compassion or indicating a shred of intelligence, there's nothing the former president can say, at this point, to shock anyone. What is there to exaggerate?

From the beginning, it's been difficult not to think of this when people engage in "resistance" cosplay, online or off. Those who oppose Trump seem just as enthralled as those who support him. So many tweets, websites, blogs, bumper stickers, memes, and books—including this one—are borne of frustration, anger, fear. Many adults call this Trump burlesque the resistance. *Look at how stupid he is,*

The assumption that sharing an image of the president's smirk with a direct, word-for-word quote highlighting his racism or cruelty or incompetence will generate political action is the same assumption one makes when sharing an image of suffering and believing the mere sight of it will end all suffering—rather than fortify the market for images of suffering.

their memes say. *Can you believe how awful he is?* their T-shirts demand. As if one hasn't already formed an opinion. The American fascist aesthetic is one of noise and merchandise: rallies and red hats, T-shirts, tiki-torches, and ideologies reduced to marketing slogans; everything superficial, cheap, stupid, and easily swallowed is prey to its usage. I wish I could say otherwise, but the aesthetic of resistance is no different—equally noisy and commodified, right down to the T-shirts, the slogans, and stupid tweets.

A marketable, usable resistance isn't a resistance at all: it's a gentrification of leftist politics that will soon discover its reliance on a fascist counterweight in order to pay its rent and keep shouting words we don't even need to listen to because they're exactly what we expect to hear. In case I haven't thus far, I want to be completely clear about this: amplifying hate, stupidity, and moral repugnance for sensation's sake does not seem an ideal way to resist a president whose only concern is fame, nor a political attitude that feeds off overwhelming visibility. Nor do many media organizations—whose marketing campaigns profess a need for support so they can explore the "truth," so they can "resist"—honor themselves by brandishing Trump's pastel face and propagating his latest threat to "democracy."

Even more astonishing is the rate at which this news is recycled into memes. Throughout 2016 and well into and beyond his presidency, Trump's words and images have been co-opted and transformed into comedy; it's a natural substitution for what is, without laughter, pure horror. But comedy belittles the threat of someone like Trump. It makes light of the fact that he exists and, even more shockingly, that he won. But in this contradictory nation that refuses to reconcile itself to its own atrocities, its own global and domestic terrorism, what needs to be resisted is the sensation of Donald Trump. Even getting rid of him cannot change who elected him—this nation that not only allowed all of this to happen, but, with its disdain for critical thinking and its worship of profit above all else, encouraged these circumstances to take root.

After the Holocaust, Adorno noted how it had become "difficult to write satire." In the wake of Nazi atrocities confessed during the Nuremberg Trials, it no longer seemed possible to strip malevolence of its political disguise: "Irony's medium, the difference between ideology and reality, has disappeared. The former resigns itself to confirmation of reality by its mere duplication. Irony used to say: such it claims to be, but such it is; today, however, the world, even in its most radical lie, falls back on the argument that things are like this . . . The gesture of the unthinking That's-how-it-is is the exact means by which the world dispatches each of its victims." When loving or admiring Hitler, say, is no longer rhetorical hyperbole but a simple dramatization of the truth, what power does the satirist retain?

Political satire is powerless when it's based on the assumption that the powerful are ashamed of their actions, or at the very least fearful of repercussions. Nor, in a system like this, can satire change the minds of those who could hold power to account. *That's how it is*, we say—those words Adorno feared. If this is what we accept, how it is becomes how it remains.

In July of 2020, when Trump was confronted with the reality of COVID-19—that it was killing a thousand Americans every day—he told an interviewer, "It is what it is."

But satire, to return to Némirovsky, is one of *Suite*'s great strengths. Even in the midst of the Reich's destruction of France, bourgeois men and women fret over what china and what linens to pack as they flee Paris. One woman, having just learned that her two eldest sons have died, performs her grief: "She drew herself up and, already imagining the black veil fluttering around her, showed her cousin the door with pride and dignity." At every turn, Némirovsky's besieged France is peopled with families and individuals who can't bear to part with their possessions or break decorum. With bombs falling all around them or with German soldiers sleeping in their homes, it's tempting to laugh at their smallness. But the novel's genius is that we don't laugh, at least not *at* these characters, not when their lives are ripped apart and irretrievably scattered: "Everything caught fire. Roofs caved in, floors cracked in half . . . Everyone was shouting at once, calling to each other, and the voices all merged into one—the village was reduced to a roar. 'Jean!', 'Suzanne!', 'Mummy!', 'Grandma!' No one replied."

No one is spared war's blood and smoke: "None of them knew why they were bothering to flee: all of France was burning, there was danger everywhere. Whenever they sank to the ground, they said they would never get up again, they would die right there, that if they had to die it was better to die in peace. But they were the first to stand up when a plane flew near." It's this precise juxtaposition of life's lightness and its sudden fragility that makes the comedy in *Suite* so affecting. In her notebooks, Némirovsky acknowledged this ambition: "If I want to create something striking, it is not misery I will show but the prosperity that contrasts with it." With village girls flirting with their German occupiers; with moments of spring birdsong in between bombing raids; with the scent of cherry blossom coming in through the windows of a bedroom a German officer has taken over; and with the attention given to choosing the right bottle of wine, the right cheese, to using the best flour or the ripest peaches, *Suite Française* is a monument to the human wish for continuity, for familiarity. Living in terror, one reads in this fiction the wish to wake up every morning and recognize even a small piece of one's world.

***

Fiction, of course, is just another casualty of a culture in which most persons responsible for that culture (writers, artists, journalists, politicians, filmmakers, "influencers," entrepreneurs, and so on) present themselves as images. If the reader's expectation is trending toward *character* = *author*, it's likely because authors have become accessible images—first as celebrities, now collected as friends or followers. Enabled by the contemporary publisher's abandonment of the author to the management of their own

brand, readers grow familiar with, even interact with, that brand: the persona associated with the author's books when seen in stores, at libraries, online.

Here, "JT LeRoy" is instructive. Albert refers to JT as her avatar, alluding to digital personifications in online role-playing games. But so too does *avatar*'s Sanskrit ancestor, अवतार (avatāra), conjure deities embodied, beings who "cross over" into visibility. It connotes a risk, an opportunity to be caught in the flesh—a risk Albert took until she was, in effect, caught. Yet it wasn't, she told *The Paris Review*, just a trick to make money: "I published everything as fiction. JT was protection. He was a veil upon a veil—a filter. I never saw it as a hoax."

And it's true that each of Albert's books was published as fiction, that Jeremiah and Cherry Vanilla are only characters. But what "JT" seems to have been is a visible incarnation of those characters—"he who crossed over" from a novel's world into this one. It's natural, pleasurable, for the human mind to make connections or identify patterns; and those who fell in love with LeRoy's books chose to see him as his characters. And nobody intervened. Nobody said, *It isn't like that*. Literature often elicits this resemblance to love, or love's shadow. LeRoy, uniquely, became someone readers could target with that love, an imitation—a fiction—of intimacy.

To impassioned fans, LeRoy wasn't an avatar. Once this image was exposed—or deciphered, or explained, or interpreted—the person readers had adored became someone else, an unmasking that never, in any relationship, goes well.

It's for this reason, I think, that contemporary writers perceive a cultural desire for fiction that is or seems to be autobiographical. It's why, I think, "autofiction" is, if not popular, a popular topic of discussion. While Smith is right to suggest a fear or distrust of colonialism, of invading another's experience and profiting as if it were one's own, the greater risk is to cast the shadow of love upon an avatar created by a person who may one day hurt you, whether they know it or not. To read fiction is to risk being moved by someone who may have done or said terrible things. It is to risk facing the wholeness, the humanity, of those whose actions may have harmed us or others. It is to risk knowing that no one can be seen as in a photograph, consumed in a glance.

To read fiction is to risk sharing, without profit, the most precious thing you have: time.

***

Honestly, the institutional isolation of American writers shouldn't be a surprise in a country where small talk with strangers begins with "So what do you do?"—a question that means, *What are you for and how does your function relate to mine?* Where are you, we want to know, within capitalism?—where can I find you on its map? In this context, "writer" or "author" is often insufficient, and we are more specifically labeled: poet, novelist, journalist, memoirist, theorist, essayist, academic, playwright, or whatever it was we borrowed all that debt to study or simulate.

Obviously this isn't law. There are many poets who write novels, many novelists who write essays, and so on. But there is a pattern, and one to criticize—particularly in the schism between "creative" and "academic" writers; or the difference that "Fine" can make in whatever Arts you're certified Master of.

Overall, any carefully cultivated specialization is isolating—

and purposefully so, not only a necessary precursor to fascism but an organizing tenet of capitalism. "Craft," in writing, is capital at work. Here's where that literary genre comes from—novels full of barking dogs, dying parents, horny professors—the kind of thing Lukács called a "caricature" of the novel, "bound to nothing and based on nothing." The C.V. novel, out of the way so one can teach others about the "tools" of writing.

"Anybody in Europe can do forty different things," as Gary Indiana once told an interviewer, "but here you're supposed to be a specialist in one thing. I find that American writers more than American artists are really provincial people. They don't mind being just writers because they live in this very clammy, creepy little world—writer's conferences and PEN and all that stuff." This isolation—the split between creative and academic on a cultural scale—is contemporaneous with the gradual disappearance of criticism from the public sphere (measured against, say, the sixties and seventies). During the Reagan years, writers seem to have publicly *turned away* from what were traditionally writers' concerns: politics, the relationship between art and the public imagination, the role of storytelling on a national scale.

Writers, in short—with plenty of help from insidious, well-financed, expertly aimed conservative propaganda—have grown cynical about literary citizenship. Our careers are most successful when we are encouraged to write our lyrical novels or self-reflective poems or personal essays; but to write exactingly about art or literature—as opposed to appraising visual or literary products for consumption—is unmarket-

As Josh Jones writes for *Open Culture*, the CIA found an ally in Paul Engle, the "self-appointed cold warrior" and director of the Iowa Writer's Workshop, whose dominance remains "lamented for the imposition of a narrow range of styles on American writing." The "rules" of writing popularized by the Iowa model, Jones adds, "have become so embedded in the aesthetic canons that govern literary fiction that they almost go without question ... What is meant by the phrase ['good literature'] is a kind of currency—literature that will be supported, published, marketed, and celebrated."

able. (Some editors admit this openly.) As Hal Foster writes in *Bad New Days*, "The relative irrelevance of criticism is evident enough in an art world where value is determined by market position above all; today, 'criticality' is frequently dismissed as rigid, rote, passé."

But criticism, Foster adds, is not merely a crucial part of the public sphere: "In some ways criticism *is* this sphere in operation." Critical writing is dialectical: by revering literature *and* holding individual works accountable to aesthetic, ethical, and political standards, it pulls the form, and the culture with it, forward and open. Otherwise, novels and other artworks simply appear. Without a multitude of accessible (read: affordable) platforms for intelligent feedback, the books one reads and the movies one sees become just another part of an individual's matrix of choices, or tastes—more commodities, more images to consume as part of one's lifestyle. And one can't produce, market, or distribute commodities in this country without participating in its profit-driven race to the bottom: of cost, of quality, of reputation, of value. Confining literature to aesthetic concerns—to craft—has been this country's extraordinarily successful and multidecade degradation of literature's relevance as a public art form.

***

It was Adorno, too, who says, "To write poetry after Auschwitz is barbaric." Often misread as an indictment, Adorno's concern is not methods of expression so much as the will toward compartmentalization that made Auschwitz possible. To pursue and create beauty after the revelations of the Holocaust is barbaric, but that doesn't mean one can't do it. It means that "barbarism"—usually a filter meant to hide whatever we don't like about humanity outside of its frame—is inseparable from our culture. Barbarism is the repulsive part of our adaptability.

Later in life, Adorno returned to this idea. In his *Negative Dialects*, he observes art's license to do what it will even in this most artless, most deathful, of worlds:

> Perennial suffering has as much right to expression as a tortured man has to scream; hence it may have been wrong to say that after Auschwitz you could no longer write poems. But it is not wrong to raise the less cultural question whether after Auschwitz you can go on living—especially whether one who escaped by accident, one who by rights should have been killed, may go on living . . . By way of atonement he will be plagued by dreams such as that he is no longer living at all, that he was sent to the ovens in 1944 and his whole existence since has been imaginary, an emanation of the insane wish of a man killed twenty years earlier.

To be happy or to pursue happiness among so much suffering is to become complicit in the creation and perpetuation of that suffering. This is what it means when "we" go on shopping, go on meeting for brunch, go on buying plane tickets, despite the bleaching of reefs worldwide, the rising of the oceans, and the annual burning of landscapes almost incomprehensibly vast. The only real end of this complicity is death, which calls to mind so many of Auschwitz's survivors—including Primo Levi, Paul Celan, and Jean Améry—who died by suicide decades after they escaped. It evokes Virginia Woolf, who never saw the war's end, or Stefan Zweig, for whom the world became too terrible in 1942.

This summary, of course—this image—elides suicide's complexity. Yet depression is immensely sensitive to external pressure. In the early-morning hours of November 9, 2016, for example, the National Suicide Prevention Lifeline experienced record surges of phone calls. It's hard not to think of all the lives we began losing to despair, after 2016. And of course it's impossible, in our era of "security," not to think of Auschwitz itself, where more than 1 million people were bureaucratically murdered, including, on August 17, 1942, Irène Némirovsky, whose *Suite Française* is still missing its final three movements.

Walter Benjamin, arrested on his way to America in 1940, gave himself a fatal dose of morphine.

Fascism trades in death. Its currency is death—hence its attraction to aesthetics, to the imposition of images. So fixed in our places, we are imagined as dead before dying; our deaths "make sense." As concerns the United States of America in the twenty-first century, here is where Schulman's distinction between conflict and abuse becomes the greatest societal urgency in human history.

The Republican party of the United States, championing Islamophobia, denying and exacerbating climate change, stripping trans and nonbinary persons of their rights, supporting police brutality against the Black community, destroying Indigenous access to ancestral land, incarcerating immigrants and separating children from their families, downplaying or subverting information about a global pandemic that has led to the deaths of hundreds of thousands of Americans—in short, committing crime upon crime against humanity, all of which is not only visible but meant to be visible—is a global terrorist organization. It sinks its roots not only in white and Christian supremacy, but the supremacy of wealth. Its hate is intersectional, and must be dismantled intersectionally— not only in identity politics, but in class warfare, or simply in the aggressive insistence that human beings across the planet have the unilateral, unquestioned right not to drown or burn or starve. To tolerate everything—or anything—that the Republican party stands for or to excuse it as "just politics" is to tolerate genocide.

We live in a misogynistic, racist, homo- and transphobic, ableist, violent, and viciously unequal country whose relatively small population (4.4 percent of the world) and vast wealth (25 percent) leave us, individual voters and protestors, responsible for the fate and future of this planet as its oceans rise and reefs die, as its air grows increasingly contaminated and water less potable. To feel so powerless and yet accountable for the future of the human race means that the sheer number of traumatized persons living in America is staggering. We are rooted in a country created by two concurrent genocides and supported by two centuries of wars, spectacular terrorism, theft, and global oppression. What's worse, as Schulman argues, traumatized persons, through their actions, amplify and spread trauma to others by shunning, bullying, silencing, scapegoating, and threatening; they cling to what little they're given as payment for their complicity in worldwide destruction at the profit of a small minority of white, wealthy men.

This is why we have learned—why we have been trained—to treat one another, to consume one another, as images. We are learning to discard and be discarded.

"Dictators understand very well," Egan writes, "that the strength of thought and analysis that literature embodies is a threat to the mind control that is an essential feature of tyranny." She's right, of course—but she may as well be describing the last several decades of American economic conditions, which are an isolating, mind-controlling tyranny of their own. Curiously, it's only because of this president that Egan's article exists, a phenomenon familiar to many magazines and newspapers. This autocratic spectacle provides a wellspring of oppositional content, all framed as necessary under tyranny, as resistance you can buy. But this is mere reaction, a marketing opportunity. Any media organization that seeks to widen its profits in the shadow of fascism will soon find fascism a desirable shadow in which to widen its profits; and any writer who stakes their value on this kind of "resistance" shrivels into a pundit.

Meanwhile, ceding to writers a vague and priestly importance, in place of criticism we get what Foster calls *fetishistic discourse*: "Any operation whereby human constructs (God, the Internet, an artwork) are projected above us and granted an agency of their own, from which position and with which power they are more likely to overbear us than to enlighten us (let alone to delight us)." By imbuing the creative author, for example, with a fetishistic degree of authority or authenticity, publishing, as an industry, leaves little or no authority to the critical author. This reverence is another flank of cynicism, a turning away from literature's anchor in our daily lives—and the renunciation of literary citizenship.

> By literary citizenship, I mean having a sociopolitical awareness of writing literature—not, say, volunteering to read manuscripts at a magazine only writers read.

And why shouldn't citizenship be a key, even radical issue for writers, as it is for everyone else? After all, no conscious person in twenty-first century America has the right to be shocked at how totalitarian capitalism destroys the individual capacity for citizenship. Do you, as an American, have time to participate in your democracy? Or is that time indebted to some other task? As a reader, do you have time to practice enriching your reading with poetry, even if you prefer biographies? If you are a writer, do you have time to give to a new kind of project—one your publisher isn't likely to recognize as part of your skill set?

From the perspective of citizenship, it *is* radical to resist not only the commodification of art, but the commodification of oneself. It's here where criticism offers a very different form of resistance: an anticynicism, a turning toward, a meeting of the gaze. There is no universal truth; but via aesthetic, political, and ethical criticism, there is dialectical truth. In the rushing flow of commodities, a dialectical approach to the art we make and the relationships we forge is the rock in the river, the stick in the spokes. Interrogating failures alongside pleasures, criticism resists reducing our works and ourselves to consumable images. Criticism fosters a sensibility of plural validation: a book is this *and* that, an author's vision successful, challenging, *and* problematic. It recognizes works and persons as existing in time and capable of change—the concept upon which all radical hopes are built.

***

Alongside an active, critical citizenship, another metaphor may be crucial. An "ecology of images," as Sontag mentions in *On Photography*—or a kind of "image control"—is a tall order in our culture, in which the image is the supreme currency. This is especially troubling in the digital era, in which the creation of images is effortless and the costs of which, no longer tied to film, are invisible. In a few years, we'll be living among ten trillion photographs, and nothing about it will feel different—we won't feel as if we're wasting our resources to take and share these images. To ask of ourselves and others, *Don't post that*, or to request that corporations scale back their image-production and dissemination, is not only unfeasible and useless but practically impossible. After all, it's not images that are in danger. It's us.

What we must imagine is an ecology of the human mind, an ecology of consciousness.

The eighteenth-century concept of rights—the philosophical and legal framework upon which many of this nation's laws are founded—is primarily positive, the right *to*. Negative rights (the right *not* to) are far harder to uphold, as the last several decades of Supreme Court decisions—many honoring "religious freedom" (i.e., the right *to* inflict ideological harm rather than the right *not* to experience such harm), corporate citizenship, and so on—have shown. In the United States, it's much harder to demand freedom from harm rather than freedom to harm, making the concept of rights something in between an antiquation and—with respect to things like the Fifteenth Amendment and Black voter suppression, or the Eighth Amendment and the sex offender registry—a fucking joke.

An imagined demand for the "right" to participate as a citizen would, in all likelihood, be met with an argument that one already has this right, provided one has enough capital to avoid working oneself into exhaustion, or that one has not entangled oneself within the criminal punishment apparatus, or that one is not Black and living in a district that suppresses Black voters, or that one has access to affordable childcare in order to go to neighborhood or city meetings, or that one simply tells one's boss "It's Election Day and I have the right to vote" without any fear, imagined or real, that exercising one's right to leave work for two hours will reflect poorly on your ability to "be part of the team"—the provisions are endless. The right to participate would, like so many of our rights, look met on paper, yet in reality succumb to the right of corporations—the heavy artillery of totalitarian capitalism—to push us into debt and poverty, to deplete us not only of the capacity for citizenship but of the capacity, as our exploitation via images has shown, for an inner life, the capacity to be a person.

Gentrification is a unique tool of capitalism. It replaces reality with a consumable image, and this is why we, too—ourselves, our politics, our art—are rapidly becoming gentrified. Totalitarian means total; its goal is total, and that includes your consciousness and mine. This is why privacy has become a luxury. It is meant to be more than we can afford, because to be private is to protect something—be it your financial information, your browsing history, your consumption habits, or your ideas, your beliefs, your thoughts, your feelings—from assimilation. It is to say that something in your life is not for sale.

Pragmatically, this means realizing that everyone requires protection from eviction and starvation, from succumbing to or suffering from easily treatable or preventable illnesses, from civic mutilation by punitive courts, from becoming trapped in jobs or careers that are exploitive, even abusive (such as Amazon's brutal regulations of something as basic, as intimate, as going to the bathroom, forcing employees to choose between disobedience and the deepest humiliation). All are protections easily and immediately provided through legislation—or taken through direct, collective action—guaranteeing universal basic income, Medicare for all, decriminalization of drugs and sex work, and cancelation of predatory debts, to name only a few examples.

We cannot afford to believe privacy is a luxury. If the capitalist ethos is to treat us as resources to exploit, we must imagine ourselves as resources to protect. While the extremely visible resistance of protests and civic disruption are crucial anti-fascist tactics, an ecology of consciousness is a daily, constant resistance—the foundation of all other forms of resistance. To demand that capitalism has no right to exploit your inner life is to realize that exploiting oneself for the sake of "resistance" burlesque is self-defeating, a sociopolitical Trojan horse. Timber, after all, wasn't irreplaceable to the companies who logged the forests; it was irreplaceable to the forests, which certainly wouldn't have logged themselves only to make signs mocking the logging companies. In the same way, we are irreplaceable to ourselves, and must demand conservation, protection; to stop capitalism's totalitarian movement, we must imagine—and demand—that our inner lives are off-limits to capitalist predation. We must believe ourselves and one another to be precious and scarce.

Irreligiously, we must believe in the sanctity of our souls.

***

A crucial word for all of us is *and*. One cannot live in moral purity, and yet one wants to live (for now). I can be afraid; I can be angry; I can be a vicious critic of a cruel administration; *and* I can spend a long weekend enjoying my life. It's hard to get through a day without thinking of the end, whether by bomb or the slow strangulation of climate change; *and*, in the summers, I spend

hours nurturing tomato plants and herbs, carrots and onions. Politically, one half of the United States government would wish to
erase the vibrancy of my gay and loving life; and, next summer,
I will meet my friends on the beach or by the pool. We will pour
ourselves a drink. We will have a beautiful day.

I wrote this book as a person, as someone worried not only
over my inner life and what was happening to it, but worried for
the lives—inner and actual—of everyone around me. It began
with images, with photography and its ubiquity, its saturation in
our lives. As Sontag writes, "the camera makes everyone a tourist
in other people's reality, and eventually in one's own." I'd begun
to see my life as a place—a destination dead as Venice, where
nothing could be changed or altered, only photographed. Then I
began to notice—that is, I began to see—how important it was,
from the perspective of those wealthier and more powerful than
me, that I believe this. That I "touch nothing" in the gallery of
my life.

"The capacity to look can no longer be seen as a personal
property," Azoulay writes, but as "a complex field of relations that
originally stem from the fact that photography made available
to the individual possibilities of seeing more than his or her eye
alone could see, in terms of scope, distance, time, speed, quantity,
clarity." Her citizenship of photography is "without sovereignty,
without place or borders, without language or unity, having a het-
erogenous history, a common praxis, inclusive citizenship, and a
unified interest." Azoulay's metaphor still seems to me of utmost
importance, as it's hard to believe in the stillness, in the immutabil-
ity, of an image if we remind ourselves to watch rather than look.
Not only does it slow our judgment, but also our consumption; we
give more of what is most precious—our time, our selves—to what
is no longer a commodity but more visibly, more understandingly,
an act of confinement, of cruelty, of reduction. To watch is to allow

the captured lives of others to better tell their stories, to establish a dialogue rather than acquire more information.

As a child, Albert didn't recognize herself in the books she read. "The characters that were allowed to have adventures and allowed to have redemption were boys, from Huck Finn to Tom Sawyer to Oliver Twist to Peter Pan. What were the girls? They were princesses." To be a girl in a book meant to be a photograph, an image that doesn't change. To be a boy meant one could grow. In her fiction, which began as phone calls to a crisis hotline, Albert translated her pain into a boy's pain, her abandonment into a boy's; alongside everything else her books did, her fiction gave her life a way to complicate itself. "I think some people take it for granted to be acknowledged and not overlooked," she added. "My experience was to be completely ignored and disregarded and disdained." When readers found out she wasn't JT, they disregarded and disdained her, and her experience, all over again.

This is what becomes of judgment in a culture—in a population—abused by consumerism. To see a person's life as the one action most marketably despised or distrusted—to make of them a victim, a monster, a martyr, anything but themselves—is to disallow that person's experience of time. It denies their capacity to change, and confines them to life as a commodity. To participate in this confinement is to carry out the will of a punitive state that sees people as its property. Whatever the social intentions, to delete or discard the stories of others, to narrow ambition to one's own identity matrix, is not justice. It is not progressive. It is a denial of recognition—that readers or viewers may confront some part of ourselves we'd rather not. It is, consciously or not, the work of the fascist imagination, and must be, like all expressions of fascism, aggressively resisted, be it in the streets or in our deepest relationships with ourselves.

None of this, of course, is to say that people—or their actions, their creations—cannot be criticized, even protested. We owe it to one another and ourselves to critique, alongside the aesthetics of our works, the politics and ethics of our lives. This *is* to say, however, that in a culture or context where it's possible to reduce one's humanity to a product, it's important to criticize that culture or context alongside the actions it fostered. Because it all flows together. In your acts and in your works, and in the acts and works of others, the risk of seeing your reflection runs in the same river as other recognitions: joy, pleasure, spirituality, longing, hope, the sublime; and fear, disgust, horror, revulsion, despair, hatred. This is your time, whether you want it or not. In that river, you'll want to tell yourself that you resisted—that you went under as slowly as you could.

ACKNOWLEDGMENTS

Pieces of this book have appeared, in very different forms, in several publications. For their guidance, precision, and generosity, I'm in immense debt to Ted Scheinman at *Pacific Standard*; Christian Kiefer and Nadja Spiegelman at *The Paris Review*; Rob Horning and Nathan Jurgenson at *Real Life*; Jess Bergman at *Literary Hub*; Allison Conner and Nathan Goldman at *Full Stop*; Dana Snitzky at *Longreads*; Taylor Davis-Van Atta and Jeffrey Zuckerman at *Music & Literature*; the editors at *3:AM Magazine*; and Jonathon Sturgeon at *The Baffler*.

So much of this book I owe to Erik Hane, who texted me and said it was about fascism; to Dan Smetanka, who endured a plague of exclamation marks sent over email like digital locusts; and to Dawn Frederick, who championed its earliest version and held a lot fewer doubts about it than I ever did.

Thank you, too, to everyone at Counterpoint for your patience and hard work while I said, over and over, "It should look like this."

I'm grateful for Joseph, Chris, Steven, Veronica, Conner, Roy, CJ, Foster, and Peter, all of whom read pieces of this book at one time or another and said, in their own way, to keep going. I'm grateful for my friends, who've helped show me how wonderful life can really be, and for my parents, who gave me that life. And I'm grateful above all for Michael, who has been more supportive than any reasonable person could ever expect.

I meant it when I said, on page 4, that I never thought I'd write a book like this. It means the world to me that I have, and I couldn't have done it without all of you.